So, You Want to be Married?

An Alternative to Dating and Perfecting the Journey to Marriage

Cornelius Lindsey

Dedication

I would like to dedicate this book to my wife, my friend, my travel partner, the mother to my children, and the woman of my dreams, Heather Lindsey.

Heather, thank you for accepting my marriage proposal. You have brought sunshine to my darkest days. You have helped me grow and see the imperfections in myself that my eyes could not see. You have been the extension of my arms when they were too short to reach. You have been by my side each step of the way, and I'm honored to continue this journey with you and our firstborn. Cheers to infinity and beyond!

Table of Contents

Introduction

So, you want to be married? You are preparing to embark on a wonderful journey that is promised to take you through some good and bad times. No matter how bad it gets, you must keep going. Trust me when I say that it can get *really* bad. Love doesn't fail, though. It bears underneath anything, and it never gives up. This is the commitment you make at the time of marriage. Are you prepared to make that kind of commitment? If not, I'd ask that you reconsider whether or not you should get married. Prepare your mind for some tough situations to come. When these situations come, be prepared to make your decisions based on the Word of God, and to be committed to those decisions.

When it comes to marriage, you must be like a tree that's firmly planted by the rivers of running waters. Your roots must run deep, and you cannot allow various storms' winds to uproot you from the plot on which you've been planted. Trust me when I say that the winds will come. You may bend, but you should not break. Your leaves may fall off, but the branches should remain. The weather may get tough, but you should not waiver. This, my friends, is marriage. With all of that being said, are you sure you want to go through with it?

I'm sure you've heard some horror stories, or you've probably seen what's happened to the marriage of someone you know, like your parents, a friend, etc. You're probably convinced your marriage will end in divorce, or you may think that everything is going to be just fine. Either way, I'd recommend that you don't marry in expectation. Don't marry someone expecting them to change on your timetable. Don't marry expecting everything to be good, and don't expect everything to be bad, either. Don't expect your spouse to be perfect, or everything you need. Don't expect roses every afternoon or lumps of coal every Christmas. Go into the marriage fully focused on glorifying God and perfecting your part in the union. If you fully focus on your part, you won't have time to critique your spouse on theirs.

Nonetheless, I wrote this book for you! I wrote this book for the man who is just curious about marriage, and for the woman who is convinced she wants to be married. Either way, this book is for you. You should fully expect to be encouraged and enlightened about the concept of marriage. This book is a compilation of mistakes I've made and learned from in my own marriage, and the wisdom that God has graced me with, that has been birthed from His mind.

I pray that this book encourages you to seek Him and seek His plans for your life. I pray it encourages you to let go of the foolish, purposeless relationships that you may be in right now. I pray it opens your eyes to a whole new world of understanding concerning marriage. I pray you don't marry an ass just because he calls himself an ox. An ass is considered an unclean beast, and can be friendly, affectionate, patient, or even sad. However, he's moody; therefore, he can be stubborn and very lazy. When I say "unclean," I mean not regenerated, or unrepentant. Marrying this type of person is like marrying a man or a woman who isn't saved and doesn't possess a repentant heart. They have no concern for their sins, don't consider Christ, and don't live in the Word of God. This is a very dangerous person. Don't make a vow to be joined in marriage with an ass for the rest of your life. They may seem playful and jolly for a moment, but only time will prove if it will last.

As you read this book, I suggest you underline things that stick out to you, and take as many notes as possible. Also, be sure to get your potential spouse a copy of the book as well. Read it at the same time and share the things that are inside of it. Study the content. Research the content. Then, live the content. Some of it will hit you where it hurts, but I know you're ready for it.

There are questions at the end of the book for you to go over with your potential spouse. Take some time and really answer them truthfully.

Well, you're on the journey now. My wife and I are excited for you.

The Beauty of Being Single

In the book of Corinthians, the Apostle Paul begins to refute the claims of some of his opponents in Corinth who say it's better for a man not to marry. Paul counters this by stating that due to the sexual immorality in Corinth, it would be beneficial for a man to have his own wife, and for a wife to have her own husband. That way, they would be able to fulfill each other's sexual requests honorably, inside the confines of a marriage union. This still holds true for the present-day. Because of the lack of discipline in many men and women, it is advisable that they should seek to marry so that they do not dishonor God in their acts of sexual immorality.

However, the Apostle Paul comes back to say that it is good for the unmarried and the widows to remain unmarried. Why would Paul say this? Well, Paul was single; therefore, he knew the advantages of being single. A single man is able to devote himself to God without having to worry about the cares and stresses of the home.

As a single man, I could leave freely and not have to worry about what I was leaving behind. I could travel the country without having to worry about coming back home to check on the welfare of my family. If I wanted to stay an extra night somewhere, I wouldn't have to ask for permission from anyone. A single man is able to devote himself to God without any distractions. This differs greatly from the married man or the father. The married man has to be sure his responsibilities at home are taken care of before he departs, and he must make sure they are taken care of while he is away. The married man, and in some cases, father as well, has a constant struggle going on inside of him. He struggles with being obedient to God while still having to care for his responsibilities as a husband and father. It is difficult for him to up and leave at the command of God, because he has added responsibilities as a husband and father.

A single man is free from cares that involve having a family; therefore, he is able to concern himself with the Lord's affairs. A single man should always be focused on how he can please the Lord. A single man is free to go stay in an impoverished country for years because he only has himself to look after while he's there. The same is true for the single woman or the widow. She is able to devote herself to the Lord without having to be concerned with being a wife or a mother. She doesn't have to worry about how she will please her husband. She is not restricted. However, the married man and the father is concerned with the affairs of this world. He is concerned with how he can please his wife and take care of his children. The married man and the father's interests are divided.

Our Great Problem

Unfortunately, we have a great problem that exists in our lives. That problem is ungratefulness. We are an ungrateful people. For example, many of the people who are single desire to be married, and many of the people who are married desire to be single. We aren't willing to be grateful for whatever stage of life we find ourselves in. We are constantly trying to find a reason as to why we feel the need to be married or the need to be single. The married man looks at the freedom of the single man. He desires that freedom to roam without permission. The single woman looks at the marriage between the married man and the married woman. She sees the beautiful children they have, and she yearns for a family of her own. Both the married man and the single woman are ungrateful. Their desires are not those originating from thankfulness. They are not thankful for the life God has already given them. They desire something more. They feel as if they are missing something.

I know many people will dispute the claim that they're ungrateful. I can see your faces now. You're probably telling yourself that you're not ungrateful and that your desire for marriage is a natural one. I'd ask you to consider this point with me: If your assertion that God is giving you a desire to be married were true, then

I would have to assume that God is a tormentor for many of you, right? I've encountered women and men alike who are so anxious for marriage that it eats away at them. They desire to be married so much that they cannot think of anything else besides marriage. That is torment. That is pain. That is not peaceful. Why would it be said that we are to seek first the Kingdom of God, which is God's way of doing things, before seeking other garbage, vain pursuits, and empty relationships? Be honest with yourself. You know that desire hasn't come from God; instead, it has come from the television shows you've watched, the movies you've enjoyed, the songs encouraging lust and intercourse, the conversations you've had with friends, the posts on Facebook, the tweets on Twitter, the pictures on Instagram, etc. I'd warn you not to attribute God to something that was birthed from your own selfish motives.

I'm sure you've heard the saying "The grass is always greener on the other side." Well, the grass may be greener, but it takes more maintenance to keep up greener grass! We like to look over the fence to see what everyone has. Then, we desire it for ourselves, negating whether or not that longing came from our hearts or it came from simple covetousness. We are ungrateful.

This issue of ungratefulness is rooted in our lack of focus, amongst other things. We are no longer focused on what's important. A single man and a single woman's focus should be kept on God the Father, God the Son, and God the Holy Spirit. A single man or a single woman should not seek marriage. Instead, seek God. Don't seek love. Instead, seek God. Don't seek sex. Instead, seek God. We must refocus on what's important and not deviate from our ultimate, singular focus, which is God. A single man and single woman's interests should be God's interests. Both the single man and the single woman should give themselves to constant interaction with the Lord. This includes constant prayer, studying the Bible, fasting, serving our Christian brothers and sisters who are hungry, thirsty, imprisoned, etc. James 1:27 NLT says *"Pure and genuine religion in the sight of God the Father means caring for orphans and widows in their distress and refusing to let the world corrupt you."* Folks, our attention should be on others, not ourselves. It's embarrassing to say, but many people trust God for salvation through Jesus Christ, yet they don't trust Him enough for His will to be done in their lives concerning their marriage or singleness.

The Issue of Lust

Now, I am very much aware of sexual temptations. They do come; however, that should not be a reason to deny God the honor He is due. If you are being tempted with sexual immorality, you should seek God. I know that is different from what others may tell you. Many say that you should seek counseling. I'm not dismissing counseling, but if counseling always worked, what need would we have of Christ? My friends, we are inclined to sin just like a lion is inclined to eat meat. You can try to train a lion to eat grass like the sheep, but he will always go back to eating meat because that's his nature. You can try to train a sheep to eat meat, but he will go back to eating grass, because that's his nature. Have you ever seen a lion jumping through hoops and putting on a show for a crowd? Well, he was trained to do it. These behaviors were introduced to him by a professional trainer, but his nature still isn't changed. He still has to be caged because he's still a beast. Sadly, many of our preachers today are trained in helping men change their actions instead of leading them to the One, who is Christ, who can change their nature. Man can help change the action of the beast. Only Christ can change his nature. Your desire for sex before marriage, drugs, alcohol, etc. is centered on your sinful nature. I could easily give you 10 steps to change your life right now, but they will only help to change your actions. You must submit yourself to God the Father through God the Son, which is Jesus, so that your nature will be changed. Now, when you hear someone say, "You must go to God in order to be changed, you should understand what that means.

Seek direction from the Holy Spirit as to where you should go and what you should do. Don't trust your own wicked heart to lead and guide you to a spouse. Marriage is all about purpose. Notice what happens in Genesis 2:18-22 NLT. It reads *"Then the Lord God said, "It is not good for the man to be alone. I will make a helper who is just right for him. So the Lord God formed from the ground all the wild animals and all the birds of the sky. He brought them to the man to each one. He gave names to all the livestock, all the birds of the sky, and all the wild animals. But still there was no helper just right for him. So the Lord God caused the man to fall into a deep sleep. While the man slept, the Lord God took out one of the man's ribs and closed up the opening. Then the Lord God made a woman from the rib, and he brought her to the man."* Notice that, initially, Adam did not find a suitable mate in the animals he named. This rules out the thought of bestiality, which is a relationship that is sexual in nature with an animal. Secondly, we notice that Adam did not go to God requesting a wife. It was God who saw the lack; therefore, He fulfilled the need. It was His desire, not Adam's. I'm sure Adam was grateful for his bride, except for when God came to punish them for disobeying the command God gave Adam. Nonetheless, it was God who saw that it wasn't good for man to be alone. This is why He provided a helpmate suitable for him. Folks, this is about God's will not yours.

A man shouldn't seek marriage just because his selfish ways cannot be controlled. Lust is a very deceptive foe; however, it is not that pressing that it cannot be overcome. The Holy Spirit can help you, and Jesus can cleanse you. Don't let fulfilling your lust be your reason for marriage. Many marriages have ended as a result of this, and only a fool believes that lust is satisfied just because they got married.

There are as many men and women struggling with pornography inside of marriage, as there are men and women struggling outside of marriage. Adultery is an offspring of lust, and it is spreading like wildfire around us. Unfortunately, lust cannot be contained, even in the confines of a sacred union like marriage. Marriage does not cure lust, and many have been deceived by this school of thought, assuming that it is true. They think that the altar will rid them of their desire to gaze at wild women and have wild orgies. It will not. The desire will still be there, and one must have Jesus to free them of that bondage of lust.

I understand that some of you are discontent with your life. You are saying, "Cornelius, I desire to be married, have a loving family and have some beautiful children." I understand your discontentment; however, the truth doesn't change just because you feel that way. I enjoy reading 1 Corinthians 7:29-31. It reads, *"What I mean, brothers, is that the time is short. From now on those who have wives should live as if they had none; those who mourn, as if they did not; those who are happy, as if they were not; those who buy something, as if it were not theirs to keep; those who use the things of the world, as if not engrossed in them. For this world in its present form is passing away."* Did you catch that? The time is short. The hourglass is slowly losing sand. We must refocus, we must refocus now. No matter what situation we are in right now, we should be grateful, and we must keep our focus on God. We shouldn't be carried away with this world. It is fading away quickly, so don't grow attached to it. Keep your focus on God, and refuse to let it change.

My Story

Before I was married, I didn't think I would even get married. First, I didn't think there was a woman out there who could put up with me. I recognized I was a handful, but what man isn't, right? Secondly, I didn't want to share my life with anyone. I was absolutely terrified of marriage. I heard all the horror stories about it, and I just knew my marriage would end in divorce, within the first year, like so many I knew of. For those reasons and many more, I didn't focus on marriage. I was focused on doing a little dating here and there. It was purely recreational for me.

I took one young lady out on our first date, to

dinner in downtown Atlanta. I knew what I was doing was wrong, but I admit that dating her was merely recreational for me. I wasn't trying to marry her. Anyway, we sat down to eat, and we did all that we could to enjoy each other's company. Finally, the bill came to the table. I confidently lifted the bill to pay it. In a moment's notice, the blood from my face rushed to my feet. Our bill was $115.00. The waiter came back to our table and asked if we wanted dessert, and I quickly told him we were fine. I figured the lemonade she ordered was enough sugar for the night. I had never paid that much for a meal for anyone, especially someone I didn't really know. These days, a bill that much is not that uncommon to me; however, back then, that was a bit much to spend, on a date that I knew wasn't going to lead us anywhere.

Finally, I got serious about my relationship with God. I began to focus on Him and only Him. I would stay up for hours studying Scripture and crying out to Him. Over time, I began to create this tunnel vision where I couldn't see anything except what God was showing me and where He was taking me. I threw myself into my work, and I concentrated on who was important to me. It was around this time that I vowed to commit myself to God no matter what happened in my life.

For months, I stopped dating and going around trying to find someone to be with me. I would see one particular young lady in New York from time to time, but I never looked at her in a way that would imply she would be my wife. I would speak to her on occasion, but I never had any interest in trying to court her. I didn't need a wife at that time. Why would a man need help if he wasn't doing anything? Adam was given an assignment from the Lord to keep and dress the Garden of Eden. Adam was given purpose and responsibility. He was in need of help. I'd like to think that Adam was lonely, not alone, because He had God. In saying that Adam was alone, one would be saying that He was there to complete the assignment, which was a daunting task, alone. God realized Adam needed something. What did Adam need? He needed help.

At the stage of my life mentioned above, I didn't need help because I wasn't pursuing a God-induced vision, nor had I realized my God-given purpose. Before going on, I must say something to the men reading this book. Men, if you're not pursuing the Great Commission, which is to go into the entire world and preach the Gospel, then your vision isn't big enough, and it doesn't warrant help. All things are to be done to God's glory. It is God's desire for all men to be saved and to come into the knowledge of the truth. (1 Timothy 2:4) To say we have the heart of God implies that we desire what God desires. Well, God desires for all men to be saved and to come into the knowledge of the truth. Is that your desire? Is that your goal in life to fulfill? Is that what wakes you up every morning? Do you think about it all day long?

Nonetheless, after months and months of staying focused on God, my now-wife and I connected. Even though I saw her countless times around the church we attended, I never thought she could be my wife. It took the Lord opening my eye, in order for me to see her that way. I wasn't actively searching for a wife. I was seeking God, and it was in His presence that he granted me favor. It was God who presented Heather to me, and I will be forever grateful.

Remember that Adam did not tell God he wanted a wife. Instead, it was God who noticed that Adam didn't need to be alone. Therefore, God created help for him. Adam did not beg God or labor in prayer for hours. Adam had enough work to do. I would like to think that he didn't have time to focus on the fact that he did not have a wife. This is the cool part! Adam had enough work to do, that it warranted him needing help. Eve was not there to just stand by his side to make him look good. She was there for a purpose. She was presented to Adam to help him. After God noticed Adam needed help, He put him to sleep, took out his rib, and made a wife. What was Adam doing while God was making Eve? He was in a deep sleep. Adam was resting. He was not in active pursuit of her. Once God was finished with the transaction, He woke Adam up and presented Eve to him. I imagine Adam standing boldly, like most men on their wedding day, saying, "At last! She is my wife! She is bone of my bones and flesh of my flesh. She came from my womb; therefore, I will call her woman. God, thank You for this precious treasure!" I love the way my wife explains the concept of faithfully waiting for God to bring a mate. She says, "Ladies, be patient because your Adam is sleeping. Don't go out searching for a husband. You may end up waking up someone else's Adam before the process has been completed in the both of you."

Are you willing to trust God to open your eyes at the right time? Are you willing to trust Him? It's silly to think that you can trust God for everything, except for Him sending you a marriage partner. I'm an advocate of a man having an assignment from God before he seeks marriage. A wife is referred to as "help"; therefore, why would a man need "help" if he's not doing anything? That doesn't make sense. Many people aren't really ready to be married. They aren't ready to grow and develop. They aren't ready to sacrifice and protect. They aren't ready to give up the pleasures and freedoms they enjoyed while they were single. You may need to admit that you aren't ready for marriage yet. If that is the case, then focus on God. Trust Him enough to show you the right mate at the right time. You may ask, "Cornelius, what happens if He never shows anyone to me?" I say, "Be thankful and serve God anyway." Our service to

God isn't contingent on whether or not He gives us a mate. We are called to serve Him and live in holiness, as He is holy. If you are actively serving the Lord, you aren't concerned about marriage anyway. If you are taking the Gospel to all the ends of the world, you don't have time to worry about marriage. If you are taking care of the fatherless, widowed, sick and poor, you don't have time to think about marriage.

Some of you may be preoccupied with worldly affairs. You are looking at the idols of this world to define your happiness. Take your focus away from this world, and focus on God. Don't allow seeking a mate to become an idol in your life. Cherish your single life and devote your service to God. Look at the beauty of being single, and be grateful that you are single. Be grateful that you can devote yourself to God without any distractions. While enjoying your singleness, learn what it means to be married. In fact, continue reading this book to find out what it means to *really* be married. For some of you, this is as far as you need to go in this book. You've made the decision to trust God and have faith that His way is much better than your own. If you feel compelled to do so, continue reading to discover what it means to desire to be married.

The Desire to Be Married

I've met many people who have had the desire to be married. Their lives were consumed with the idea of sharing their life with someone else. As I previously stated, I didn't share that same sentiment; simply because I didn't think I could ever be married. I didn't think there was a woman alive who would marry me. I knew I was a tough cookie, so the idea of being married was too much for me to consider. Nonetheless, there are countless men and women around the world who strongly desire to be married. Unfortunately, many of them have no idea what they really desire. Some confuse the desire to be married with a desire to no longer be lonely, to be loved, to feel appreciated, to have sex, etc.

Many of these desires we seek from a spouse can only come from God. He must be your first love and the main object of your affection.

First Corinthians 7:7 says, "*I [Paul] wish that all men were even as I myself am [i.e. unmarried]. However, each man has his own gift from God, one in this manner, and another in that.*" Paul draws a clear distinction between those who have the gift to remain single and those who have a very strong desire to be married. Paul realized the desire was real, partially because of the actions of many of the people in Corinth. We must realize that these issues still exist today, and I would argue that the desires are even stronger today because of the advancement of technology.

There are many young girls who love playing house with baby dolls, kitchen sets, etc. while their brothers are trying to jump off the top of the couch with their favorite superhero toys. The little girl watches how her mother and father live, how he holds her, how she talks to him, and the dynamic they both share – whether it's good or bad. Many times, she begins to desire the same type of marriage, or one that's much better than what she experienced.

For a single person who desires to be married, the internal and external pressure can sometimes become too much for one person to handle. The external pressures can come from a parent, friend, co-worker, boss, etc. who continue to ask the annoying question, "When are you getting married?" or "When are you going to get into a relationship?" Some try to answer and say that they're waiting on God to send the right person, but oftentimes that response is met with heavy opposition. The person may not understand the order or timing of God, or it could be that they just don't care about it. Usually, they will advise the single person to begin to go out on the town or to try a dating service. Some people even use Scripture to back up their views. Whatever the case, it is important to realize that our focus cannot be on getting married; it must always remain on Christ.

I sat down with a young man some time ago and he was very adamant about wanting to be married. I could sense his passion. Unfortunately, I had some bad news for him. His passion, although it was great, was placed in the wrong thing. He had forgotten about his allegiance to Christ and his duty to continually share the Gospel with others. He was only concerned about meeting a woman who could one day be his wife. While he was out and about, he would focus on finding a wife instead of sharing Christ with a lost soul. Even in relaying how I felt about his situation, the external pressure he was facing was too much for him to stand under, and my advice paled in comparison to what he was facing. He was being questioned about his sexuality because he wasn't married or actively involved in a relationship. His parents were telling him that they wanted grandchildren, and he felt great pressure from them because he wasn't meeting their expectations.

There are many people who experience that kind of external pressure, but there are also others who experience some real, internal pressure. For singles who desire marriage, the internal pressure can be more than what they might expect. Many begin to ask themselves questions like, "Does God not want me married?", "Does God just want me to be single?", "What's wrong with me?", "Are my standards too high?", "Should I lower my expectations?", and "Am I not getting out enough to meet people?". The internal pressure can be great and, in many ways, internally damaging. It can cause great loneliness, shame, guilt, and self-condemnation, etc.

Both forms of pressure are difficult to experience. I'm inclined to believe that pressure increases with age. I've met many singles in their 30s, 40s, 50s, and beyond who desire to be married. The external pressure coming from their peers and family is a lot for them, because the issue of age always comes up. In addition, a woman is usually confronted with the idea of not being able to have children because her eggs will stop producing in her 30s. It's usually easier for a man to be single in his 30s and 40s. Society might consider him a "player" or just a "bachelor." It's usually a little different for the women.

Either way, the pressure may seem like too much to deal with at times. Here's the thing: I don't have all the answers, but I do know one thing; I know that God makes no mistakes, and life isn't worth living if you have to continue questioning the decisions you make, or have made. In fact, the single person needs to focus on Christ rather than the fact that they are single. I mentioned this in an earlier chapter, but I think it's worth mentioning again. Paul writes to the Corinthians *"Are you married? Do not seek a divorce. Are you unmarried? Do not look for a wife. But if you do marry, you have not sinned; and if a virgin marries, she has not sinned. But those who marry will face many troubles in this life, and I want to spare you this. What I mean, brothers, is that the time is short. From now on those who have wives should live as if they had none; those who mourn, as if they did not; those who are happy, as if they were not; those who buy something, as if it were not theirs to keep; those who use the things of the world, as if not engrossed in them. For this world in its present form is passing away. I would like you to be free from concern. An unmarried man is concerned about the Lord's affairs-how he can please the Lord. But a married man is concerned about the affairs of this world-how he can please his wife—and his interests are divided. And unmarried woman or virgin is concerned about the Lord's affairs; Her aim is to be devoted to the Lord in both body and spirit. But a married woman is concerned about the affairs of this world—how she can please her husband. I am saying this for your own good not to restrict you, but that you may live in a right way in undivided devotion to the Lord" (1 Corinthians 7:27-35).*

I know that was a lot, but it really drives the point home, and it eliminates the pressure. Paul instructed the Corinthians to be content in whatever stage of life they were in, whether single or married. He instructed them to be free from concern, and to focus on the Lord's affairs instead of focusing on their marital status. I'm inclined to believe that we should do the same thing in our lives.

It is vital that you focus on the Lord's affairs rather than continue to be focused on your marital status. I know some single people who can bake really well. I instructed one young lady to use her baking skills to bake cupcakes. She wanted to know what to do with them because she didn't have a husband or children who could enjoy them. Do you see her focus? She was so focused on pleasing her one-day husband and children that she was no longer focused on pleasing the Lord or those who are less fortunate. I instructed her to take those cupcakes to an orphanage and to donate them to the children there, or take them to a home for the elderly and bless the residents.

James 1:27 says, *"Religion that God our Father accepts as pure and faultless is this: to look after orphans and widows in their distress and to keep oneself from being polluted by the world."* I shared this verse with her, and explained to her that this life is about more than just being married and having children. This life is about being fully concerned with the affairs of the Lord, and we know the Lord's affairs have to do with His children all over this world. After hearing this, the young lady was joyful, because she felt like she had a purpose again. She was excited and on fire again, because her focus had changed.

The same type of excitement that the young lady felt can be yours today. I want you to realize that your desire to be married isn't a bad thing. It's a great thing to desire to be married; however, the desire cannot overcome you. You cannot allow the desire to become an idol in your life. That is a big mistake that you cannot afford to make.

Actions We Take

There are many people who go to many different places trying to find a spouse. I've heard of women going to church to find a spouse. They think the best men are the ones found in the church pews patiently listening to the sermon that's being taught by the pastor. Unfortunately, that's not always the case. Usually, the churches are saturated with a ton of women. Young women who are passionately in love with God usually dominate the young adult scene, but the shockingly low number of present, young men over the age of 20 is troubling. Because the number is usually so small, the women settle, and rush to get the next available guy she notices. She practices spooky things like telling a man God told her to marry him or wearing tight-fitting clothes to draw his attention. Ladies, using your clothes to draw him will work against you. If your bait is perverse and unholy just think about what kind of fish you're going to catch. Take a moment and dwell on that.

Some people try going to the gym or to the park. They try wearing very revealing clothes to attract someone that doesn't need to be a part of their lives. Folks, if you dress like bait, there's very strong potential for you to end up on the wrong hook! You have to be careful and consider what you're willing to show, because someone will think that what you're willing to show, you're willing to share.

I know people who pray consistently for a husband or a wife. They journal daily to God about what they want in a spouse. They spend time writing down certain characteristics about what they want their mate to look like and what they want their mate to do. Or, there are some who keep journals where they actually write to their future husband or wife.

I want you to really reconsider how you look at waiting for a husband or a wife. Writing to them at this stage of your life could make them seem real before you've actually met them. That's not always a good thing. That can quickly turn into a fantasy world that takes you much too far out of reality.

Make no mistake about it—faith is not fantasy! Faith is dependence on God; fantasy is a false world created by human imagination. Faith and fantasy don't mix well. It's like trying to mix oil and water. You can keep stirring, but they still won't mix. Faith places you in great expectancy for God's will to be done in your life, while fantasy makes you feel as though you have already attained it. What I'm saying is that you should continue to live by faith and keep your focus on God's will for your life. Look forward to marriage and the children you'll one day share. Continue to have faith in God for all those things, but don't spend your days allowing your mind to live as if the future is your present.

We are to be thankful for our present, rather than being concerned about the future. God takes care of the flowers, the blades of grass, the animals in the wild; how much more will He do for you, seeing that you are His child?

In praying, pray that God will send you someone who is cultivating the fruit of the Spirit. Long hair and great abs are awesome for a moment, but they are insignificant in comparison to Christ-likeness. Pray that God sends you someone who challenges you to be better, rather than encouraging you to continue loving the world and all that is in it. You'll do yourself a disservice marrying someone who is interested in being in the club, going to parties nightly, drinking, lying, stealing, and cursing, etc. Instead, you want someone who is consistently working towards Christ-likeness every day. You want to marry someone who is committed to dying to themselves daily, and not allowing "self" to rule them. Pray for Christ-likeness above all things, and believe that God will present to you a spouse who will meet your physical *needs*, and not your selfish wants.

Never forget that marriage is a self-sacrificial relationship like the relationship between Christ and the Church. **Take a moment to read Ephesians 5 then come back to the book.**

Ephesians 5 should've shown you the importance of walking in love, wisdom, and the light. The chapter also helps you to understand the responsibilities that wives and husbands have toward each other. Lastly, this chapter helps you to appreciate the great love and high esteem our Savior has for His Church. It's definitely a powerful chapter, and it should be one you and your spouse read over and over again during your courtship and your marriage.

You'll notice that what you read in Ephesians was totally different than what is portrayed on television nowadays. Folks, reality television doesn't define our society or the way we live. Only God and His Word define our society, our lives, and the way we live. Never forget that.

Don't get sucked into the marriages you see on

television or the ones you see in certain movies. The greatest romance novel is the Bible. It's filled with great drama, but it's all about the love a Father has for His children. I'd advise reading the Bible as your romance novel, instead of reading something that is going to take your mind and focus away from Christ. He must be your first love, and the object of your affection.

In this time of singleness, there are a couple things that I recommend that you do. I'll list them.

1. Focus on Christ.

2. Focus on loving and serving others as you would the Lord.

3. Begin to learn more about marriage. Find some great resources on marriage, and study them. Begin to work towards Christ-likeness with the help of the Holy Spirit. Listen to messages and read books that focus on you denying self and serving others. Marriage is all about dying to self, so begin to learn about it and practice it daily.

4. Turn away from this world and forsake everything that is in it.

5. Meditate on these verses about marriage.

   a. 1 Corinthians 7; Ephesians 5; 1 Corinthians 13:4-13; Romans 12:1,2; Genesis 2:18; Genesis 2:21-25; Genesis 1:27,28; Hebrews 13:4; Isaiah 54:5; Revelation 19:7-9; Revelation 21:9-14

Where Do I Start?

So, you want to be married? Well, I'd recommend first being complete while you're single. However, I don't want you to confuse being single with being alone. Being single does not mean that you are alone. It means that you are unattached from marital commitments; however, you are wholly dedicated to God.

Being single is not a bad thing. It isn't something you should avoid like the plague. In fact, it should be celebrated. A single man or woman doesn't have all of the responsibilities that a husband or wife does. A wife is tasked to make sure her house is tidy, food is prepared, the children are together, etc. A husband is concerned about staying in communication with God so that he may lead his family. He is concerned about protecting them from both carnal and spiritual attacks. He is concerned about providing for them, loving them, and acknowledging them. The husband and the wife must devote their time to paying attention to the needs of each other, and that isn't an easy job. However, the single man or woman has but one responsibility, and that is to serve the Lord. The husband and the wife must find time to pray, serve, give, commune, laugh, worship and dance with God. The single person can do it whenever she or he feels like it. I could go on and on and on; however, I'm sure you get my point.

Being single is not a sentence of loneliness. It's a powerful time of devotion and service to the Lord. Don't you dare think that being single means that you must be lonely! How can you be alone when God is omnipresent? That means that He is everywhere. You cannot run away from His presence. You cannot escape His love. There isn't a valley deep enough, or a mountain high enough to keep Him from you. He is there with you right now. Embrace Him. Many people assume that

God presented Eve to Adam because he was lonely. That's not correct. God told Adam He wanted to provide him a helpmate that was suitable for him. God stated that it wasn't good for man to be alone. Being alone doesn't mean that he was lonely. How could Adam be lonely seeing that he was there with God? God didn't present Eve because Adam was lonely. He presented Eve because Adam was in need of help. This is why God referred to the woman as a helpmate. Eve was purposed for help, not to be the filler for loneliness.

I know some will say, "Well, I want someone here with me physically." That means that you want someone to hold you, cuddle with you, run fingers through your hair and pleasure you. I've definitely been there in my life. Sleeping in a king-size bed is only fun for so long. Sooner or later, you want someone to come and join you; lay with you; caress you. Cold nights are perfect for such romance; however, they don't fulfill the void that's in your heart. You must realize that you cannot cure being single, because it is not a disease. It is a perfect relationship between a man, or woman, and God.

You've never thought of it that way, huh? Did you

ever think that being single really meant you were in a relationship? Probably not. That's because you see being single as being lonely. Television shows and songs all portray being single as a disease or something that you should avoid. However, the Apostle Paul was single, and he was quite pleased with it. In fact, as I previously stated, he recommended that all the single people remain single, if they would be capable of avoiding sexual immorality. Paul writes that it is good for a man not to marry or have sexual relations with a woman in his letter to the Corinthians. However, he cites a very interesting problem that might cause many men and women to marry. He cites the problem as being sexual immorality. Paul didn't want man to indulge in wickedness, wrongdoing, lewd acts or impurity through sexual intercourse. So, he offers a solution. The solution is that man should marry and have his own wife so that he can freely extinguish his sexual passion in the boundaries of God-ordained marriage. Sounds simple, right? Well, why do we make it so difficult?

I ask young men to read 1 Corinthians 7, so that they can tell me the main idea concerning the chapter.

They all tell me something about marriage; however, Paul only mentions marriage as a solution. He doesn't offer it as the recommendation. Instead, he actually offers being single! Can you believe it? You're running from the very thing Paul is saying is more beneficial.

I know you're bored. You're lonely. You're depressed. You're hurt. You're hiding behind a façade, and you think marriage will cure it all for you. Unfortunately, it will not. You will go into the marriage with the same issues you had while you were single. Unfortunately, you're also bringing someone else's problems into the marriage, along with your own. There is a reason why you are so lonely and depressed. There is a reason why you associate being single with being unhappy and lifeless. It is because you are idle.

I've always heard that an idle mind is the devil's playground. I believe it to be true. Being idle is a dangerous thing. Have you ever washed dishes before? I know I've washed my fair share of them. After you wash the dishes, it is vital to drain the water out of the sink. You don't want it to stay in the sink for too long. Why? Because it's idle, and anything idle begins to decay.

Think about all of the bacteria that is decaying and forming in that sink. Sooner or later, it will begin to stink. Nothing is moving. Everything is staying the same. In order to stop the stagnation, you must drain the sink of the water; thus, it must move.

Have you ever heard the saying that a rolling stone gathers no moss? That's a true saying because as the stone rolls, the moss cannot grow on it. However, if the stone doesn't move for a long period of time, it can become covered in moss.

You must get active! You have to get moving! You must not be idle! There is so much for you to do when you're single. You can travel the world and tell other people about Christ. You can leave when you're ready without asking for permission from your spouse. You can buy what you want, when you want, without asking for permission. You can eat what you want. You can say what you want. You can literally do whatever you wish to do, within reason. You are not bound to a spouse. The only authority you have is with God. That is a treat for a single man or woman; however, many don't realize it. They run to dive into a relationship thinking it will cure their loneliness and depression. You don't need a relationship to do that. You need to get moving. You need to get active. You need to get busy. You need to roll and dust off some of that moss. You need to drain your sink of that dirty, decaying water. You need to keep moving, and make sure that you don't look back.

My wife and I have a great friend who lives in the Middle East, and she travels. She is always on the move; therefore, she rarely gets bored. She is in amazing places, meeting amazing people, and doing amazing things. She doesn't have time to think about marriage. She doesn't have time to sit and think about someone holding her at night. She is happy to be out enjoying her life, and serving the Lord.

Marriage can be an idol. It can pull you away from your relationship with God, but don't let that deter you. Marriage can also be bliss. Marriage is exactly what you make it. You can make a beautiful masterpiece with the right strokes of love, forgiveness, patience, and fun. Don't be in a hurry to get married. It's work! It's beautiful, but it's work! So in the meantime, get active. Stay active. Do some of the things you've always wanted to do. Go to another country, volunteer at a local animal shelter, start that business you've wanted to get off of the ground for years, or simply begin that fitness regiment you've been putting off for years.

Marriage is a gift, so don't try to steal it; don't barter for it; don't sell your soul and body to obtain it.

The Basics of Marriage

Deception of Independence

We live in a society where women are being taught to despise marriage and family. Different artists create songs urging them to be more industrious and independent. They're told to look after themselves, and to not depend on anyone to assist them. They create a very individualistic mentality that keeps them in bondage to the world. The idea of independence is troubling, and it goes against the ways of God.

In 1999, an all-woman group came out with a song encouraging women to have men to pay their bills. Then, in 2000, they came out with a song urging women to be independent. This song urged women to defy any authority from a man, seek man's presence only when they're lonely and destroy the God-ordained structure in marriage by saying that it should be 50/50. Many young women where seduced by this song and many others like it.

As a result, women have fought for independence from men, and equality in marriage. I hate to inform the prideful that it is not God's will for a man and a woman to be equal in marriage. 1 Corinthians 11:3 says, *"But I want you to understand that the head of every man is Christ, the head of a wife is her husband, and the head of Christ is God."* You can flip it, change it, or deny it, but the truth of it will never change. Man has been given authority by God to be the head of his household and the marriage. A woman or a child should never seek independence from man. In fact, man, woman, and child must all work together for the greater good of the family.

I do understand that many men have perverted their authority. They throw around their headship as if that gives them the right to be rude and abrasive. That's wrong! Ladies, I would caution you to never entangle yourself with a man who has a heart that has not been regenerated, which means that his heart has yet to be changed by God. Ladies, this type of man is dangerous. If you are not careful, he will use religion to put you in bondage, and he will also attempt to use it to run his household. This type of man is not truly saved; therefore, he leads with a position of perverse power, and God is not pleased with his authority. Even though these conditions are present in many households, a married woman is asked to show her husband, who does not have a regenerated heart, the love of Christ by exemplifying it in the household. She is expected to show him love and patience, and to be submissive. To do simple things, like cook him breakfast and dinner, run his shower so that when he gets home it's nice and hot. Uplift him with respectful words like "I appreciate you" and "I respect you." Show him the love of God through you. Do that as your reasonable service to God.

Ladies, you were never meant to be independent. In fact, Christian marriage is likened to the union between Christ and the Church. The woman in the union is the Church. That should excite you! From this, you should see that Christ would never want you to be independent of Him. Christ only wants what is best for the Church. He protects the Church; sacrifices for the Church; gives to the Church. He doesn't abuse the Church; mistreat the Church; misguide the Church. Before you seek marriage, consider the man who is courting you. Make sure the patriarch, or the male figure who is supervising your relationship, is watching what this man is saying and how he is acting. You don't want to marry a man who will completely destroy you. Especially since you now know that behavior like that is not how Christ would behave towards you.

Ladies, throw off this independent armor that you've put on. Refuse to accept the world's idea of how marriage should be. You do not want to go into your marriage thinking that you must be independent. You don't want to go into it thinking your money is your money, your things are your things, your body is your body, etc. You need to have the mindset that the marriage is a complete blending of the two of you. What was once just "yours" becomes "ours." You are no longer allowed to be selfish. In fact, selfishness cannot exist in a Christian marriage.

Boys to Men

I'm sure everyone is aware of this one thing, but I do think it is worth being repeated. Men nowadays aren't really men. They are merely boys whose bodies never stopped growing. Think about it like this; I'm sure you have seen a little boy try to pick up something that was too dangerous for him to handle. You quickly took it away from him. You did that so he wouldn't hurt himself. Unfortunately, the little boy never learned the lesson. His child-like mind still exists; even inside a growing man's body.

Now, the little boy who used to be 5 has aged to be 26. Not much has really changed for him mentally. The only thing that has changed is his body. He hasn't "grown up", so to speak. This little boy in a grown man's body recognizes that he has a penis. Like a child, he runs from playground to playground showing it off to people and using it haphazardly. He hasn't learned the purpose of why he has it, so he abuses it like he does all of his other toys.

Our men have been babied. Our boys walk the street, defy authority, and go through life without any real purpose. Our boys are lost, and, sadly, many of them aren't trying to find any example to follow. It is so easy for someone to tell them to follow Christ, but I say, "How can a boy follow Christ when he has no clue who Christ is?" We allow television and video games to babysit our boys. These things teach them how to drive, shoot, and curse. We send them to public schools to be taught by men and women who don't reverence God or His ways. They go to lunch with foolish children who deny God. They hang around with older guys who influence them to do terrible things. We give them so much freedom, that we don't realize we are doing more harm than good. We don't meet their friends. We don't talk with their teachers, or at least meet them, to ensure that we're comfortable with them. We don't talk with their coaches. We don't screen their video games. We have left them to be taken care of by society, and we have created a big group of babies parading around as grown men. Sadly, our women have had to step up to lead. They have to care for the children the men leave behind after they've helped to create them. They have to run the household because the man isn't prepared or willing to do it. They have to run the churches because men refuse to go to them. Our women have had to pick up our slack for far too long.

Men, we can no longer seek to be babied by society. We must mature. We must mature by presenting ourselves as living sacrifices to God and being transformed by the renewing of our minds to God's will. (Romans 12:1,2) We must not seek our own ways. Instead, we must conform to the ways of God. We must learn God's ways and teach them to our wives and to our children. We must learn to care for our responsibilities. We must come to a point where we, ourselves, realize that we must mature.

I was on the road preaching in Little Rock, Arkansas when a boy walked up to me and said he wanted me to meet his girlfriend. The boy had to be about 15 years old. I didn't get a chance to see his girlfriend, so I'd rather not speculate about her age. Nonetheless, I asked the boy this question: "Are you thinking about marrying her?" He looked at me, and he said, "No!" with big eyes and a lot of frustration. He was confused as to why I was asking him that question. Then, he said, "I'm not ready to be married. We're just dating." I was floored by his response. I couldn't help but think that the world had gotten to him too. He thought it was Biblically sound for him to date this young lady without any intentions of marrying her. I quickly sat him down and explained what the process of getting ready to be married was, to him. You could tell that he just didn't know. He was doing what everyone around him was doing. I remember asking him if he was financially or spiritually ready to care for a wife. His eyes were huge, at this point. He had no clue that all of this went into marriage.

Men, we must recognize that our desire to be married must honor God. Marriage cannot be centered on a selfish goal. It must be sound, sure, and from the Lord. Before we even think about marriage, we should consider whether or not we are financially, spiritually, and physically ready for marriage. We cannot seek to be joined in a union with a woman when we don't have ourselves together. You should want your prayer life to be sound before you enter into a marriage. I have never needed God, in my entire life, as much as I have needed Him in my marriage. Marriage will bring many difficulties, primarily because you have to kill your selfish ways. It's not always easy to die to our selfish ways. We want things how we want them, but marriage confronts those selfish desires head on. Marriage will show you all the areas in your life where you go wrong. I thought I was perfect before I got married. After I got married, I realized I wasn't nearly as perfect as I thought I was. I was selfish, envious, pious, lazy, perverse, etc. Marriage put a mirror up to my face and showed me the ugly truth, whether I wanted to deal with it or not. Many men run from the marriage because they don't want to see what's in the mirror. I ask you to consider what your motive for getting married is. You can say that you are lonely, depressed, want to have sex, etc., but none of those things are right. The only reason a man should get married is because God directs him to be married, and God presents the man a bride just like He presented Eve to Adam. There's no other reason. A man is to be led by God in all things, *especially* marriage.

The Truth about Submission

Many women are disheartened when they hear the words "Wives should submit to their husbands." Some women cannot stand to hear those words. The very thought of submission is troubling to them. That's because society has sold this idea of freedom, and freedom represents no submission of any kind. With freedom, a man is able to worship a cow if he so chooses. A woman is able to kneel before a picture of a cat if she so chooses. Freedom is deceptive. Christians do not live in this world's freedom. Our freedom is in Christ. That means freedom for a Christian is within the boundaries of love. We freely do things, with love as our motivation. With love as our motivation, we won't kill, steal, or destroy. I don't have to worry about killing or lying to my brother if I truly love him. See, the Law provides man boundaries on how he should worship. Love, which is the completion of the Law, provides man with the true heart of worship. When we are motivated by love, we will freely submit.

Our issue lies in the fact that we do not love as Christ commands we love. As a result, we error in how we view submission. Many men do not realize that we are called to be submissive as well. Men are called to be in submission to Christ. We are told to humbly submit ourselves under the hand of God. That means we no longer have our own ways, dreams, goals, etc. Instead, we focus on the mission directly given from God.

Wives aren't the only one of the two told to submit. Yet, many people do not realize this great truth. I pray these next set of sentences open your eyes to the truth and release you from bondage.

Now, if a husband is submitted to the mission of God, he will strive to love his wife as Christ loved the Church. Therefore, a wife could peacefully submit to her submissive husband and bring pleasure to the Lord. Most marriages are built on the foundation that the wife is the only person who has to submit. That's not correct. Many marriages are also built on the foundation that only the wife must serve her husband. That's also incorrect. Paul says, *"But by love serve one another."* (Galatians 5:13) It is the husband's responsibility to serve his wife and seek her best interests. It is the wife's responsibility to do the same for her husband. This means that the husband should be willing to jump in the kitchen and wash dishes or cook the food. He should provide for his wife when she's sick in bed. He should be there to help serve her, and be sure her best interests are his ultimate goal. This is how Christ treats His Church.

Submission is a complete yielding to another's desires without resistance. It means that you put yourself "under a mission." The prefix "sub" means under, so it would be "under mission." Yield means to give up; to surrender; to give up one's place; to concede; to stop resisting. Submission to another's wishes is an attitude of the heart done willingly. One the other hand, slavery is done by force. Submission is done by your own will. The Apostle Peter writes that we should submit to civic authorities, parents, God, etc. (1 Peter 2:13-25).

I want you to imagine that your marriage is a house. Let's say that the foundation is God the Father, the husband is the upstairs, and the wife is the downstairs. In a submissive home, the foundation, the upstairs, and the downstairs can all coexist. However, if the downstairs refuses to submit to the upstairs, the house is divided, and a divided house is sure to fall.

Our resisting against authority is wicked, perverse and derived from the enemy. We must understand that submission is birthed from God. In marriage, both the husband and the wife must submit unto the Lord. Here's the thing I love about God: He never forces us to submit. If He did, it wouldn't be submission. It would be slavery, and God is not a slave-owner. Slavery says, "You do as I say because I'm your master." Submission says, "I ask you to follow me, in love, because I first loved you."

A husband should never demand that his wife to submit to him. A wife should submit to him because of the love, leadership, and honor he bestows upon her. We can observe that another level of submission in marriage is a wife giving up her last name to take the last name of her husband. That's the right thing to do. I'll never forget sitting in the courthouse with my fiancé, at the time. The lady sitting across the desk was asking us questions about marriage; then, she asked, "Heather, will you be taking Cornelius' last name?" Heather paused for a second, and looked at me as if it was a multiple-choice question. My eyes got big; then, I saw Heather smiling as if she was trying to pull a joke on me. I didn't think it was that funny at the time, but I see the humor in it right now. Nonetheless, I would've been gravely disrespected to have a wife who didn't take my last name. The last name symbolizes more than just marriage. It's a lying down of one's identity, to assume the identity of another. Taking on the husband's last name is godly. I wouldn't dare counsel a woman not to take her husband's last name. For a woman to refuse to take the last name of her husband is rebellion. She is trying to hang on to the identity she had before she got married, and it's wrong. It doesn't matter how prestigious the last name is or if it is a famous heirloom. Accepting her husband's last name is the right thing to do. We, as the Church, assume the last name of Jesus. This means we take on His identity, not that we are called by a set name. It also means we are united with Him when we're baptized in His name.

Submission is a beautiful thing. It's beautiful to see a wife put down her own interests, willingly, so that she can merge with her husband's. A wife should recognize her husband as the priest and head of the family. Her submission is a powerful thing that will bring great success to the family. Endeavor to have a relationship submitted unto God. Don't try to copy anything outside of how God designed for it to be done. Outside of God, everything is total rebellion. A husband and a wife should never have separate interests that divide them, and both of them should submit to God in everything, as they submit to one another by the grace of the Holy Spirit.

I remember my wife asking me to wash the dishes one day. I was furious because I didn't want to do them. I felt like washing dishes was a woman's job. I'll never forget God saying to me, "Washing dishes is not gender-specific." That stung, in the core of my being. I quickly jumped to my feet and started washing those dishes. I'm not saying washing dishes became a law to me. I'm saying that I was led to wash them because of my love for God and my bride. I washed them on my own will. I wasn't forced. She didn't have to beg. I washed them out of my love, and that is a great and reasonable service.

Please understand that the marriage will require

some give and take. Be willing to give a little extra to make sure that the best interests of each other's desires are taken care of; however, don't seek to always satisfy each other's selfish desires. This leads me to my next point.

Selfish Desires

A dictator wants to please himself and only himself. He rules from a position of power and fear. A Godly man doesn't seek to please his own interests. Instead, he seeks to please the interests of his wife. Marriage is not purposed to meet your own selfish, worldly desires. I had a man ask me if it would be okay for his wife to perform oral sex on him. He stated that he liked it; however, she didn't want to perform it. He said he asked her to do it out of the love she had for him to make him happy. I stepped back for a second to think about what he had just said, and I was flabbergasted. This man was using his wife to meet his selfish desires. He wasn't seeking her best interests. He didn't have her best interests at heart. He didn't care that she was uncomfortable doing it. In fact, her reasoning for being uncomfortable with performing oral sex was valid. The mouth was created for eating and talking – amongst other righteous things. Do you know what we call any situation that misuses the purpose and intent of a thing? We call it perversion. Our society accepts a lot of things like gay marriage, bestiality, divorce, etc.; however, that does not mean it's not perverse.

I had another young man, whom I disciple, state that he wanted to get married. I asked him why, and he said, "Because I want to find a wife who can do stuff that I want her to do, but I don't like to do; like cook, clean and do the laundry." I was sure the young man didn't have a clue as to what he was saying, so I explained it to him. It was evident from his response that he was double parked in the twilight zone. That's a joke. Nonetheless, he wanted a wife so that she could provide for his selfish desires. He didn't want to be married to help her in any way. He desired her presence so she could be his slave. I counseled him to get a maid instead of getting married.

You must understand that marriage isn't purposed to meet all your selfish needs. If it were, it would be called idolatry! A husband must be focused on loving his wife, and a wife must be focused on submitting to her husband. There is great truth in why this is special for any marriage.

Purpose of Marriage

The purpose of marriage is singular in focus. The purpose is that the husband and the wife might become conformed to the image of Christ. The marriage is purposed to destroy all of the selfishness in the two of them, and to create an image of grace, mercy and unconditional love. Those of you who desire to be married should begin to practice grace, mercy, and unconditional love with everyone you come in contact with daily. It will be needed in your marriage. Those are the top three, basic ingredients for a marriage. I must also inform you that you cannot give what you do not have; therefore, you must have grace, mercy, and unconditional love in order to give it to others. You cannot have it unless you have Christ, and you cannot share it unless you do it by the grace of the Holy Spirit.

I'm confident your marriage is going to be a

blessed union. Please make sure you get married for the right reason, and by now, you know that the right reason is because God has called you to be married. The callings of God are irrevocable. That means that God will never take that calling away from you. Therefore, there's no reason to discuss divorce because it's not an option. I would assume that the men reading this book have a feeling they have been called into marriage. If that's the case, prepare to lay your life down for God. In doing so, you will lay it down for your wife and your future family.

Now that you understand marriage, let's discuss the process of searching for a spouse.

Searching for the One,
or the Next One

I figured this book would not be complete if it didn't have anything in it about the idea of searching for "the one" or even searching for "the next one." I bet you're wondering what, "the next one" is, huh? Well, the next one is for those individuals who have been married before and are interested in being married again. There are different reasons for someone to be looking for the next one. It could be that death separated you from your previous spouse, or it could be that your marriage ended in a brutal divorce. Either way, it's vital for everyone to understand that the idea of remarriage isn't a bad one.

We must realize that divorce is no longer something we see in movies. Divorce has made its way to the pews, the choir stand, and the pulpit. Christians around the world are divorcing one another for one reason or another. Nowadays, there isn't a Christian family who hasn't felt the bitter sting of divorce either directly or indirectly. We must realize that marriage is not a social contract that can be torn up at will. I know the world thinks and says that divorce is okay, but Malachi 2:16 tells us that God hates divorce. We may see it as an option, but God still hates it. We no longer see marriage as a promise made in our vows as we state, 'Till death do us part." Instead, it is a pledge based on the two people staying together "as long as they like each other."

With the presence of prenuptial agreements, rising divorce attorneys in our communities, and "no fault" divorce laws, marriage has become an all but sought out remedy for our selfishness and refusal to love our spouse as God has loved us.

I'll never forget riding down the street and seeing a sign stating that a marriage could be dissolved for

$299.00. On top of that, it stated that the marriage partner did not have to be present to make it official. I was saddened, but not surprised. That spoke volumes as to how we, as a society, have come to view marriage. It's almost like it's been whittled down to a form of elementary schoolyard-type love.

You must realize that divorce is man-made and not divinely ordained. The Bible does not record the institution of divorce after the fall of Adam as a part of human society. Divorce is a great representation of man's rejection of God's original plan for the cohesiveness of the marriage union. Marriage was never intended to be dissolved. There's no point in time where Christ divorces the Church; however, man has accepted the idea that it is okay for him to divorce his wife.

Usually, we begin to develop our passionate views about marriage based on our experiences in life. I've been asked questions like "Is marriage worth it when you're living in a home that has no love?" I understand there are some tough times and situations for certain people in their marriages, but it doesn't grant a person the right to divorce. We understand that love bears anything. Think of the vilest of all actions that your husband or wife could commit, and then realize that love still loves in spite of that vile action.

Listen to how Jesus responded to the question of divorce. It's written in Matthew 19:8 "Jesus replied, "Moses permitted you to divorce your wives because your hearts were hard. But it was not this way from the beginning." This proves that divorce has never, and will never be God's plan for His children. The fact that Moses allowed it doesn't mean that God instituted it. God allowed Moses to allow it so that the situation didn't go from bad to worse.

We all realize the pain and the shame that comes from divorce. We realize that many generations have been affected because of divorce. Children are emotionally damaged because of divorce, and many families are ruined as a result of it. We must realize that divorce is not, and will never be God's plan.

Nonetheless, divorces have taken place. For those who have gotten a divorce, realize that the divorce is final. Your moving on and abiding in Christ is what's important now. For some of you, you must release the anger and hatred in your heart towards your ex-husband/ex-wife. You cannot continue to hold back forgiveness from those who need it from you. It's poisonous to operate this way, and you must rid your heart of this.

If you are reading this book, I'm going to assume that you are interested in being remarried. Understand that in the Bible, the primary purpose of the divorce procedure was to make sure the husband did not remarry his former wife once she was remarried. (Refer to Deuteronomy 24:2-4 and Jeremiah 3:1)

Your desire to remarry is fine; however, you shouldn't seek to remarry your former wife if she has already remarried another man. For those who strongly desire to remarry, I'd recommend that you go back to the previous chapter and reread it. Afterwards, come back and continue reading about, "The next one."

The Next One

Well, you've already been married. You should be one up on the person who has not been married, and that's a great thing. You should know what to look for and what not to look for in a spouse. Many of you are probably asking God the question as to whether or not He has the "next one" ready for you to marry. I'm sure you want to know if someone is out there for you, and I'm sure these thoughts cross your mind daily.

Ladies, I'm sure you imagine lying down in a pasture alone only to have a strong, valiant man run atop a hill to lie by your side. There, he softly caresses your hair and tells you that you're beautiful. He cuddles up close to you, wrapping his masculine arms around you. A sense of protection radiates through your body, and you begin to drift off to sleep in amazement of the sense of peace you have experienced just because of his presence. Do you think of that? Do you, ladies? I'm sure many of you do; however, we all know that life doesn't necessarily happen that way.

We must realize that God is an awesome God. He has created wonderful children, and, most importantly, He gave all of His children a choice. We have the choice of whether or not we want to follow Him, follow the devil, lie, cheat, or steal, etc. The choice is ours. God is not a slave master. God does not, and will not force you to do anything. You must make the choice. The reason I'm talking about choices so much is because it's vital when discussing the process of choosing a mate.

People are everywhere, and you have a choice about whether or not you want to marry any of these people, or not.

Now, I know that this next example might be horrible, but I'm going to use it anyway. Imagine that the world was a giant buffet. There would be all different kinds of food on that buffet. Some of the foods you'll like, and some you won't like. You select what you like while getting rid of, or ignoring, what you don't like. It is somewhat similar when choosing a spouse.

This world is filled with beautiful people of different shapes, sizes, ethnic backgrounds, personalities, etc. Settling for one person isn't what you should do. Instead, you must allow God to make presentations to you. I loved how God presented Eve to Adam.

I love how certain marriages have been brought about because two people allowed the will of God to be done in their lives. They were two ships flowing down the same current headed towards the same Lighthouse. There were no special things the ships had to do. They were only focused on getting to the Lighthouse and staying there.

Folks, you and your future spouse are the two ships. The Lighthouse is Christ. You shouldn't be focused on trying to get the other ship's attention; rather, your focus should be the Lighthouse.

Upon reaching the shore, there will be many ships at the dock. You don't have to go with the first one you see. Allow the Spirit of God to lead you and guide you to a right one. Either way, there will be much work ahead.

You've been married before, so this process should not come as a surprise to you. Trust God. He's the creator of all things, so don't you think He's wise enough to order your steps in relation to your next marriage?

The One

Now, let's talk to those of you who have yet to be married. I've been in several relationships that did not end so well. I was involved in one serious relationship that was off and on for about 7 or so years. It was a verbally abusive relationship where I did most of the abusing. My tongue was as sharp as a sword, and I was unable to control it. I said many things that I now regret, and I did many things that I also regret.

Nonetheless, our last exchange was a defining moment for me. I was saying that I was one with Christ at the time, but I wasn't living solely for Him. We went to a restaurant she worked at so that I could try the food. On the ride back home, we had a conversation about her being my top priority. I told her that couldn't happen. My priorities were God, my family, my job, and then her. She didn't like the answer, so she asked to be taken to her friend's house. Upon pulling up to her friend's apartment, I told her if she got out of the car this time, it would be the last time, and that the relationship was over, and there would be no reconciliation. Well, she got out, and that was one of the best decisions she ever made—in my humble opinion. Her getting out allowed me to focus more on God, and opened up the opportunity for me to meet my wife, Heather.

I told you that story because I, at one time, thought my ex-girlfriend was the one for me. I assumed she was the one I would marry. We went to the same high school and university. Our families were well acquainted with each other. It just made sense to me. It came easy to me. I figured I just needed to make it work. I was preparing to force something that could've very well worked if I would've chosen to love her as Christ loves the Church.

Please make no mistake about it. I'm more than pleased with my marriage, and there's nothing in me that desires to have anyone else but my wife. I said what I said because I want to show you how I had a choice in the matter. I could've very well made her a priority over God and served her as if she was a god. That would be foolish, right? However, men and women do it daily. I chose not to make her a god in my life, and, ultimately, I chose not to make her my wife.

I understood the choice was mine to make while still realizing that God had a plan for me. It wasn't until I met my now-wife that I understood what that truly meant. I'll never forget talking to Heather, my wife, as we sat down to eat for the first time. I knew in my heart that God designed her just for me. She was more beautiful than any woman I had ever seen. Her skin glowed as if the sun shined on her all the time. Her beautiful smile lit up the room. Our conversation was edifying, and I could tell she was all about purpose.

At the close of the evening, we walked back to the place I was staying at in Manhattan. She had to go to the bathroom. While she was in the bathroom, the Lord began to deal with me about how I was going to end the evening. After a lengthy conversation with the Holy Spirit, I was told not to kiss her until our wedding day.

As she walked out of the restroom, I told her what the Lord told me, and she smiled. I realized she agreed with me, without me even saying it, that the relationship was headed towards marriage. It wasn't that she was the only one for me; rather, it was that I chose to make her the one I would marry for my lifetime.

Please understand that I believe I was led by God to marry my wife. I believe God presented me with her. I believe it was God's will for me to marry my wife. And, I believe it was my choice to marry her.

Ladies and gentlemen, don't get caught up in constantly searching for a husband or a wife. Don't get caught up in making that an idol in your life. Instead, spend your time focused on pursuing God with everything in you.

I love the verse of scripture in Proverbs that reads, *"He who finds a wife finds what is good and receives favor from the Lord."* Some of those who are divorced may argue that what they found wasn't that good, but let's not harbor ill will towards them. This verse is powerful because it really paints a wonderful picture of a man receiving favor from God because of the treasure he's been given. Also notice that the verse implies that the wife is a precious treasure, who is meant to be found. The question is "Where is she hiding?" I've heard several people say that a woman should be so deep in God that a man has to go to Him in order to grant permission to speak with her. Now, I don't argue that point; in fact, the man should go to God anyway.

God treasures women so much! I want you to look at it like this; God the Father places the woman under the protection, love, and care of her earthly father from the time of her birth. If her father is missing, God the Father becomes the father who stands in his place.

At the time of marriage, the woman goes from the covenant protection of her father to the covenant protection of her husband. The father literally "gives her away" to her husband. The husband and wife then grab hands and the wedding begins.

We cannot make light of the significance of the father giving his daughter away to her husband. This is a transfer of leadership, stewardship, love, compassion, protection, care, etc. from one man to another. At no point in time does God, the Father, leave the woman open to the enemy. He has her covered at all times. She is safely hidden in the protection of her earthly father or the protection of God the Father in her earthly father's absence.

When a man makes a woman his wife, he assumes

a type of responsibility that is second to none. It's very significant, and it cannot be overlooked. He must realize that she is a treasure that is precious. At no point should it be tainted by the ways or schemes of this world. Where is she hidden? I believe it's in the bosom of God the Father, and the arms of her earthly father. We all know that fathers aren't perfect, and their arms cannot reach as far as God's. Women, take comfort in knowing that where your earthly father's arms cannot reach, God's arms will extend.

Purpose-Driven Relationship

So, you want to be married? Let me ask you a question. What's the purpose of marriage? The answer to that question is vital as it relates to your desire to be married. We should know that the marriage union between a man and a woman is a great representation of the marriage union between Christ and the Church.

We should understand that marriage is the place for sex, and is only there to serve its rightful purpose in marriage. Marriage is purposed for love and glorifying God. It's purposed for dying to self and unconditional love.

I know many people who choose marriage as their

answer for their lust. They soon find out that marriage will not quench the desire of lust that seeks to take over a person's soul. I know many people who choose marriage as their answer for loneliness. They soon find out that although marriage will provide them with a mate, it won't fill that void of loneliness that's only meant for God to fill. People choose marriage for one reason or another. Ultimately, we should choose to marry because we understand that it's a divinely-created union that glorifies God.

Oftentimes, we get involved in certain relationships and we don't understand the purpose for the relationship. Think about some of the relationships that you may have right now. Do you really understand the purpose of the relationship? Do you really understand why you keep hanging out with that person? Do you understand or know the purpose for calling that person? I'm sure we all have an idea of what we think the purpose of the relationship may be, but has that purpose been communicated between both parties, and understood?

There was a young man who reached out to me

looking for some advice about a relationship with a female friend that he was involved with. He said that the two of them were "just friends", however, he was beginning to, "catch feelings" for her. He realized that she wasn't acting as if she had the same feelings, so he didn't know what to do. I asked him this question. "What's the purpose of the relationship?" He responded and talked for about 20 minutes, but he never answered the question. So, I asked it to him again. Finally, he said, "I don't know the purpose of the relationship." He realized that he was just continuing a relationship that had no purpose, and as a result, one of them was bound to pervert it.

You see; if you fail to know the purpose of something, you're bound to pervert it. If I don't know the purpose of gasoline, I can very well drink it. If I don't know the purpose of a pen, I could very well try to eat it. The purpose of something is extremely important, and it cannot be skimmed over. Knowing the purpose for each of your relationships is vital for the overall success of those relationships.

I enjoy sitting down and asking the Spirit of God to

tell me the purpose of particular relationships. Then, I like to ask my friends what they think the purpose of the relationship could be. Afterwards, I discuss the purpose of the relationship so that neither of us perverts it by thinking the relationship is more than what it is meant to be.

Although terrible, this next example should help everyone understand how vital purpose is to relationships and provides an example of a deeper truth. I had a buddy of mine, many years ago, who would tell women that he didn't want a relationship; he just wanted sex. He was wrong, and thankfully the power of Christ has compelled him to change his ways.

My friend was having sex with a certain young woman, and he made it clear to her that he was only interested in the sex, nothing more. However, she began to develop feelings for him. She told him that she fell in love with him.

Both of them knew the purpose of the relationship was sex, so it was easy for him to remind her of the original reason for the relationship. In reminding her, she understood what happened, but she was still madly in love with him. She eventually began to stalk him, and it didn't end up being a good situation. I never understood the problem, seeing that she was well aware of the purpose from the beginning of the relationship. Years later, the Holy Spirit finally confirmed to me the issue that both my friend and the young man I mentioned earlier had in their respective relationships.

Here's the thing; you learn to love what continues to give to you. In both instances, someone in the relationship continued to receive something from the other person. What confused boy #1 and girl #2 was the fact that they fell in love with what was continuously given to them.

Boy #1 fell in love with the attention he was receiving from his female friend. He fell in love with her presence, and the fact that she was there for him when other people were not. Girl #2 fell in love with the sex. For her, it became more than sex. It was a way for her to feel appreciated, loved, needed, wanted, secure, beautiful, and sexy. She knew the relationship was only supposed to be sexual, but her longing for security, purpose, and identity quickly grabbed a hold of the first thing that came her way. It was like a tick that attached itself to the first animal with fur that came to provide it with food.

Her desire for any form of what she thought was love grabbed a hold of the sex and began to suck it of its life, like a tick would suck blood from a dog. My buddy tried to tear her off just as one would remove a tick from a dog, but he couldn't seem to get rid of her. Eventually, they got it worked out, but only because she jumped onto the next unsuspecting subject who showed her the slightest bit of attention.

You see, purpose is extremely vital. It's important to communicate the purpose of the relationship with the other person so that everyone will be on the same page. It's also important to repeat the conversation, to make sure everyone is on track.

Consider the relationship we have with Jesus. We know Jesus' purpose was to die for our sins and to reconcile us back to God the Father. Our purpose in the relationship is to receive and confess Jesus as our Savior and Lord. We receive and confess Him as Lord and we commit our lives to serving Him in word and deed. This is the purpose for the relationship we have with Christ.

Many of us have to be reminded of the purpose of the relationship so we will know our role and how we should act. Remember, if you don't know the purpose of the relationship, you're bound to pervert it.

I've met many people who don't understand the purpose of their relationship with Christ, so they begin to pervert the relationship. They begin to ask Him to fulfill the requests in their vain prayers, and to support their selfish ideas. They look to Him to do things that are outside of His nature or His intended purpose. We treat our perverted relationship with Christ the same way we treat our other relationships. Since we don't know the purpose of those relationships, abuse is inevitable.

Consider an Olympic athlete. She wakes up very early in the morning, trains 2 times a day, 4 days a week, for almost 6 hours a day. She commits her life to training for one event that could, in many ways, change her life. I wonder what would happen if we treated our journey to Christ-likeness, just like this Olympic-hopeful treats her training for the event. Take a moment to think about it; then, continue reading. She doesn't party, drink alcohol, overeat, or lose any sleep. She misses family activities, television shows, and outings with her friends, just so that she can go to bed early to get an adequate amount of sleep. She remains disciplined because she knows the purpose of why she's doing what she's doing.

We should all understand that purpose is the reason why something is done or why it is created or why it exists. Usually, our relationships are not governed based on purpose. They're governed based on feelings. Many of our relationships are just adolescent-based, faux-marriages.

Let me explain. They're based on immature feelings, and they're conducted as if the two have already been married. The girl likes the boy because of his muscles. She feels like he might make a good husband because he looks good. She doesn't realize that looks can be very deceiving. She gets involved in a relationship with him, and they begin to kiss and have sex as if they are already married. After a couple years of this type of activity, they decide to just move in together without making any kind of commitment before God. Neither of them clearly understood their purpose. If they did, they would've realized that they were going in the wrong direction.

Ladies and gentlemen, be sure you sit down and talk to your prospective spouse about the purpose of the relationship. Talk about the purpose of marriage. Talk about the purpose of the engagement. Talk about the purpose of the courtship. Talk about the purpose of sex in marriage. Talk about the purpose of having children. Discuss all of these things to make sure that the both of you understand the purpose of the relationship, so that you don't pervert it.

The Dangers of Dating

There is a new phenomenon that has hit our society. It is called dating, and everyone is doing it. Dating has turned into a huge money-maker. Now, we have television shows dedicated to dating. We have internet dating sites, speed dating, and music that encourages it all over the world. Unfortunately, the Bible doesn't say anything about dating.

I realize there are many happily married couples whose marriages are a result of dating, but I want you to understand that there is great danger in dating. I'm not referring to courting or a betrothal. I'm referring to worldly dating, which consists of premarital sex, deep emotional connections, a great deal of kissing, and heavy petting, etc. This system of dating is recreational in nature, and it has no real purpose besides fulfilling lust, loneliness, and perversion. Never forget that it's satan who convinces us to fill a legitimate need, illegitimately. Nonetheless, let's examine some of these dangers now.

Lack of Purpose

We've already discussed this in depth, so there's no need to continue digging in it. It's important for you to understand that dating doesn't always come with purpose. Oftentimes, we don't have purpose for the relationship, so we fail to identify the ending. When we fail to identify the ending, we prolong the inevitable. Let's move on.

Emotional Connection

A connection is a relationship in which a person, thing, or idea is linked to, or associated with something else. It is a linking from one thing to another. In dating, the connection is between the emotions of both individuals in the relationship. Emotional connections are achieved when one of the two people involved in the relationship begins to admire or like qualities in the other person, and vise versa. Or, an emotional connection occurs because there is a giving or sharing between the two individuals, usually of intimate things. Remember reading in the last chapter that we normally fall in love with what continues to give to us? Well, this holds true for emotional connectivity in dating.

The danger begins when the emotional connection is not being monitored, watched, or guarded by a rightful authority. A child shouldn't be given a knife because she or he is too young to properly handle it. It's dangerous to give a child a knife. That doesn't mean that the knife is bad; it only means that the child should be supervised to make sure that they don't hurt themselves.

The same is true for dating. A father should look at his daughter as if she is a precious treasure because, honestly, she is one. He should not be willing to allow some young man, no matter how clean cut he may appear, to be alone with his daughter, because he might say things that are not edifying or glorifying to God.

Usually, the two individuals involved in the relationship will begin to behave like teens in love, laying important responsibility or obligations aside so that they may pursue a relationship built on the foundation of feelings and emotions. The foundation of the relationship is based on the condition of what he or she likes about the other person. There is great danger in that kind of worldly view.

We notice that God does not ask us to like our neighbors; instead, He commands us to love our neighbors as we love Him. Our society is infatuated with the idea of liking someone. Let me ask you this question; how many people have you "liked" or been "in love" with, before this relationship you're involved in right now? Consider all the other people you've been involved with that you "liked" or "fell in love" with in the past.

The problem with "falling in love" is that usually the person who falls in love finds some way to fall back out of it. I had a young man tell me that he fell out of love with his wife. I laughed for a second, and I responded, "Well, find that hole you climbed out of and fall back into it."

Love is not some trivial pursuit that you can just fall in and out of. It doesn't work that way. Love is everlasting. It bears all things. It doesn't quit or stop. Stop reading this right now, and go read 1 Corinthians 13. I want you to begin at verse 4 and read the entire thirteenth chapter, then come back and finish reading, here. You'll notice that you just read about pure love. This is the type of love that can't be fallen in and out of. This is pure love.

One of our biggest issues is that we seek to satisfy feelings rather than fulfill purpose. As I stated in an earlier chapter, our purpose is to please God, and we know that we please Him by faith according to Hebrews 11. Our faith should not wavier in the area of relationships. We should purposely have faith that God will meet our needs and provide a spouse in accordance to His will and not our own. Many people in this world are seeking the wrong things. They're seeking a wife or a husband when they should be seeking God. Matthew 6:33 says *"Seek ye first the Kingdom of God and His righteousness and all these things shall be added unto you."* We completely miss that, and we focus on seeking relationships rather than seeking God. We must know that God has to be our first priority today, tomorrow, and forevermore.

Protection

Dating doesn't provide protection. Oftentimes, dating involves a less restrictive relationship where the two people involved are only accountable to each other. That's extremely dangerous! It's dangerous because the two people involved are depending on their flesh, and worldly way of thinking to sustain them in the relationship.

They're depending on will power to stop them in the heated moment of lust. Unfortunately, they do not realize that will does not have power! It's easier for a man to give birth to a baby, than it is for a man devoid of Christ to stop lust when it pledges to wage war in his body.

We live in a society where we turn away from protection. We dislike having anyone instruct us or tell us when we're wrong. We don't like counsel, and we turn away from the protection that an elder or wise counsel could give to us. We are rebellious at heart, and that rebellion destroys us from within.

Has your earthly father met the man you say you love? Has he sat down to really talk to him to see if he is good enough for his daughter? Have you at least told your earthly father about this man?

Men, have you alerted an elder, your pastor, a deacon, or your earthly father about the woman with whom you're involved? Have you taken her to meet your wise counsel so that they may communicate with her to see if she is who you say she is? Many times, we are blinded by lust, and we call it love. Wise counsel and godly protection helps us to not be consumed by our inability to see past our lust-glazed eyes.

Restricts the God-Ordained Right for Parental Involvement

The Bible is very clear that children should respect and obey their parents. We live in a society where children are almost praised for going against their parents. Parents no longer discipline their children, so the children grow to despise authority and submission. The very heart of respect for authority and submission is grown in the child by how she or he respects his or her parents. Parents are to discipline the child and teach them about respecting authority, starting with respecting them.

Ephesians 6:1 says, *"Children, obey your parents in the Lord, for this is right."* Colossians 3:20 says, *"children, obey your parents in everything for this is pleasing to the Lord."* Exodus 20:12 says, *"Honour thy father and thy mother: that thy days may be long upon the land which the Lord thy God giveth thee."*

A parent's words should carry much weight when they are in line with the ordinances of God. However, if a parent's orders go against the words of God, the child has an option in whether or not they will follow those rules. For example, we all know that God has told us not to steal. If a parent tells the child to steal, the child is not obligated to follow the orders given by the parent.

My wife and I are big believers that a relationship should have a group of seasoned advisors that advise and provide protection for the two people involved in the relationship. The advisors are there to provide emotional and physical protection. Emotional protection is about guarding the heart so that neither of the two people involved in the relationship are saying anything or making promises that can have a negative effect on them later.

The physical protection is watching how they talk to each other, how the two look at each other, how the two touch one another, and where the two go alone. Before marriage, the two people should have very little alone time together to avoid the appearance of evil, and to lessen temptation. The advisors are there to help read body language, and to listen to what the two are not saying, just as much as what they are saying.

Practice for Divorce

Worldly dating is recreational in nature. It causes people to get accustomed to breaking up each time the relationship gets difficult. Each time you end a useless dating relationship you're communicating to yourself that it's okay to quit when times get tough and hard.

Think of all the relationships that you've ended in your past. Think of the reasons why the relationship ended. Whatever the issue was, it was nothing love could not bear; however, I'm sure you were very passionate as to why you ended the relationship. Continuing to do it could promote emotional fornication and provide a rehearsal for divorce.

Impossibilities or Uncertainties

There are some serious things out there. Nowadays, you don't know who has been with whom. You don't know who has HIV or other STDs, etc. You don't know if the person you meet online is an online stalker or a serial killer. I'm not trying to provoke fear in your heart; instead, I'm trying to get you to focus on Christ and your continued trust in Him.

Many times, dating creates an illusion of marriage. It makes you think the two of you are already married, so you begin to act as if you are already married. Sadly, many relationships are controlled by illusions, which are false ideas or beliefs. It can be a deceptive appearance or impression that we may have about someone who doesn't really feel the same way about us. Your reality becomes skewed and you begin to think and act based on deception.

The 'love bug' has mesmerized many. Cupid's arrow has pierced many hearts, and now they're living in a fantasy world. There are also some serious emotional stresses that come as a result of being dumped, in a relationship.

The Alternative Suggestion

Instead of continuing to date the world's way, consider this. Consider engaging in a relationship that promotes and respects certain fundamental values, including parental authority, parental protection, moral purity, creating boundaries regarding affection, and a God-centered understanding of marriage.

Initially, make sure you understand the purpose of marriage. We discussed this earlier. Also, be sure that you understand the purpose of why you are engaging in this type of relationship. Let your purpose be God-driven rather than emotion-driven. Usually, we seek to satisfy emotions and feelings first. Once our feelings and emotions fizzle, we try to seek purpose. We begin to ask questions like "Why am I even in this relationship anyway? "Why do I allow them to treat me like this?" "Why do I care about them so much?" You must be focused on purpose *first*, before even considering your emotions or feelings.

Secondly, make sure God, your parents, elders, leaders, and/or advisory council approve the relationship. You must understand that you are only able to see so much. Your father, an elder, an uncle, your pastor, etc. is able to see something in the other person that you may not be able to see. They can read the person's body language, listen to what she or he isn't saying rather than what she or he says, and ask questions that you may not think to ask.

A spiritually mature advisor, whether it's a parent, an elder, etc., can see things in this person that you may not be able to see. The Spirit of God can tell them something that you're not opening up to hear. Oftentimes, we can become so involved in the relationship that we allow certain things to go over our heads without properly addressing them.

For example, let's say you're courting a young man and you two start arguing over something simple. In a fit of rage, he grabs you by your arm and threatens to hit you. After about an hour, he calms down and apologizes. Because you're "in love" with him, you dismiss it, as if it didn't happen.

Let's say that you didn't inform anyone about the altercation. About a year later, you marry him as if it never happened. One night he comes home late and you begin to interrogate him about where he's been. He gets upset and grabs your arm again, even though he said he would never do it again. This time he takes you and throws you against the wall and places his hands around your neck. That's a very scary situation to be in, but it's one that could have possibly been avoided. By informing your father, an elder, a deacon, etc., you could've asked them to have a talk with him or asked them to help him find help for his anger. There is great protection in submission. Don't run from it.

Thirdly, consider the relationship as valuable. When we understand the purpose and value of something or someone, we usually tend to take better care of it. Men, realize that she's not your girlfriend. Get rid of that adolescent mindset and stop using those childish terms. She's God's daughter, and your sister in the Lord. Her body is the temple of the Holy Spirit, and no man in his right mind would seek to defile the place where the Spirit of God lives.

Would you defile the Ark of the Covenant by debasing it with unclean blood and perverse things? I don't think you would. Therefore, don't seek to defile the temple of God, which is our body.

Women, he's not your boyfriend. He's God's son. He's a bond-slave to the Lord. His body is the temple of the Holy Spirit, and no woman in her right mind would seek to defile the place where the Spirit of God lives. You're both valuable to God, and neither of you should seek to defile His temple. Treasure yourself as you would God's earthly vessel because, in fact, you are His earthly vessel.

Since the relationship is valuable, spend precious time educating yourself on what is acceptable, and what is not acceptable in the relationship. Spend precious time communicating by asking a lot of questions. Spend time with groups of people instead of being alone, to lessen temptation.

Spend a great deal of time around married couples with marriages that are symbolic of the marriage between Christ and the Church. Be mature about your relationship and your answers. If the purpose is unclear or if it has been diluted, it may be a mature decision to end the relationship.

If something does come up where your father, an elder, your pastor, etc., recommends ending the relationship, strongly consider it, depending upon the source you receive that particular advice from. If something happens in the relationship, and you realize this is not God's best, be mature about ending it. Have a discussion about the dissolution of the relationship, and move on.

Ending a relationship is much easier when you're not emotionally connected. This is why it's important that you don't involve the emotions in the relationship until you know without a shadow of a doubt that the person will be your spouse. There's no reason to invest your emotions in an account that doesn't promise great interest or a great return on the initial investment. Be intentional about the relationship, and make sure you remain protected with sound, biblical advice.

Instead of thinking about "playing the field," consider being committed to one person. Dating advocates exploring your options to determine what it is you want in a mate. Biblical courtship focuses on reserving all of your emotional and physical intimacy for one person, your spouse.

Instead of trying to form a deep connection, consider focusing on real commitment. Dating assumes that you should know all there is to know about this person before making a commitment, marriage, or that you should know this person more deeply than you do anyone else in the world.

Courtship promotes real commitment, and it stresses that real commitment precedes a high level of intimacy. This will lessen the amount of your heart you give away to undeserving people. Dating puts intimacy before commitment. As for you, consider placing commitment before intimacy.

Instead of focusing on having your own needs met, consider ministry and service to God and meeting the needs of others. Dating assumes that the relationship should "meet all my needs and desires." This is self-centered and not biblical. Courtship suggests that the relationship should be a ministry and service unto the glory of God. It has no foundation in self-gratification.

Instead of focusing on high intimacy, consider little to no intimacy in your relationship. Dating is all about a high level of emotional connection with a person, and that you should assume that there will be some physical involvement, i.e. kissing, touching, sex, etc. Consider not having any close physical intimacy, and very limited to zero emotional intimacy outside of marriage.

Instead of trying to make your relationship private, consider spiritual accountability. Dating says that who I date and what I do when I date someone is my business. Courtship says that there is a level of spiritual accountability in which I allow others to see my actions so that they can be encouraged or criticized. Your desire should be to mature and get better, and you can only do that by standing and living in the light.

Instead of trying to "find" the right person for you, consider "being" the right person. Dating is all about "finding" the right person for me. Consider "being" the right person to meet your future spouse's needs, and being one who glorifies God in the marriage.

Lastly, instead of acting like you're already married, consider really getting married. Dating is all about acting like you're already married. If you like it, it's official. If you don't, then you'll just have to separate. Consider not acting as if you're already married before the day actually takes place. You're not to act as if you're in a marriage-level commitment until the commitment truly exists before the Lord.

You must recognize all the dangers that exist in dating. Use wisdom, obey your parents, and maintain a wide range of wise counselors to help lead, direct, and supervise the relationship.

Waiting

Let's dive deep into the concept of waiting until marriage. When thinking about waiting until marriage, we think about sex. As in most situations, it's the first idea that pops up in our mind. However, I want you to go a little deeper with me.

It's no secret that our society is inundated with sexual images. We are bombarded with different ideas and concepts of how to please our flesh. Our minds are filled with ideas of how we can satisfy our deepest, most intimate desires no matter how dangerous or perverted. I know this from personal experience. With all the advertisements for fleshy satisfaction, our standards and morals have eroded—some, faded completely away. We have become a people filled with corruption and hatred for what is pure and excellent. With all that being said, where does this leave you and the idea of waiting until marriage?

I'm sure you've heard many people give reasons for the importance of not engaging in sexual intercourse until marriage. While I agree with them, I'm not going to discuss that here. Instead, I want to bring your attention to a deeper matter in relation to waiting until marriage. Consider a man and woman preparing for marriage. Nowadays, it's common for them to engage in all manner of sexual intercourse before walking down the aisle to enter into wedded bliss. They spit on the sacred institution of marriage by living as if purity isn't important or even necessary. Please understand that these words aren't intended to condemn; however, they are definitely written to convict.

While controlling our sexual desire has a part to play in waiting until marriage, it doesn't sum up the entire idea of what it means to wait. The physical investment of sex is only part of it. The other part is the emotional investment. Sadly, we've become accustomed to investing emotionally in every relationship we enter. Then, we leave fragments of ourselves in all of our previous relationships—both physical and emotional. I want to encourage you to consider yourself as a whole entity rather than a fragmented one. This means that you are not just some sexual piece—a prostitute walking the corner waiting to open your legs, or a dog in search of his next hump. You also have a mind that is capable of doing more than conjuring up more mischief.

Waiting for marriage is as much about the emotional investment as it is the physical one. My wife and I created boundaries so that we wouldn't do anything we would later regret. By God's grace, we were able to save our first kiss for our wedding day. While the kiss was special, we were also able to save a lot more. When we got married, we were able to invest in one another emotionally. Our communication was deeper and richer because we chose to consider the sacred bounds of marriage.

I definitely was not a saint before I met my wife, but I refused to use my past as an excuse to live like a godless fool in my present and future. Be encouraged to save yourself for marriage. For those who never get married, save yourself. Remember that your body is not your own. It is the edifice in which God resides. Don't dare pollute His sacred temple with perverse, lustful activities that lead to death and condemnation. Remain accountable, and stay focused on inheriting the crown that doesn't tarnish or wrinkle.

The Vows, Engagement and the Ceremony

The Vows

I know you probably will not want to admit this, but we spend more time focused on the ceremony than we do considering the significance of the vows of marriage. The average person could easily tell you the ending of the traditional vows. We know them to be as follows; *"I (insert name), take you (insert name), to be my (wife/husband), to have and to hold from this day forward, for better or for worse, for richer, for poorer, in sickness and in health, to love and to cherish; from this day forward until death do us part."*

For most of the world, those words mean absolutely nothing. You may say, "How can you say that, Cornelius?" I don't have to say it. Just look at the divorce rate. Think of all the people you know who have gotten a divorce in your family or in your friend's family. Many people's entire lives have been shaped adversely as a result of divorce. Generations have been destroyed because of divorce. It's a real part of our society, and it cannot be ignored.

We understand that our hearts are hardened because of sin. We are estranged from God, and only Jesus can bring us back into unity with Him. Because of the hardness of our hearts, we have a very difficult time keeping our word. It's no secret that we have a huge integrity problem in our society. This is evident of many affairs. Man has a difficult time keeping his promises, or vows, and allowing them to remain true.

The vows should reflect the sacred promises the two of you share with each other. They should properly reflect the couple's union with each other, the marriage, and God, and fully capture the identity of the union. Each of our journeys is different, but the end result is the same.

The vows should reflect the journey, but most importantly capture the significance of the end result. There's nothing wrong with allowing your vows reflect your personalities, hopes, faith, and creative use of the English language, or whatever language you speak. Just make sure they capture the seriousness of the situation.

When I got married, I wrote my wife a poem. I'll admit that it was a little funny, but I made sure I captured the seriousness of the moment. I mentioned some stuff that was specific to our story and our journey. It made the moment extra special, and added an extra touch to an already blissful situation, seeing that it was about to be the first time I kissed my wife.

Vows should not be empty words. They are meant to be taken seriously. Vows are the heart of the wedding ceremony. I'd suggest taking some time and truly reflecting on the vows before saying them. Sit down with your potential spouse and read them to each other over and over again. Meditate on the words, and make sure you understand the sacred promises you're making before God and man.

This will help you in moments of your marriage when you want to give up because it's too hard or you just don't feel like going on. It helps you to remember the vows and to choose your words carefully when you're upset. I'm confident you'll have some "for worse", "for poor", and "for sickness" times. You'll need to remember those words for those times. You'll also have some "for better", "for health", and "for wealth" moments. Marriage is full of great surprises, and it's a big adventure to take with a person for a lifetime. Therefore, make sure you truly consider the vows you make before God, because they're binding.

The Engagement

I'll never forget Christmas of 2009. I had my family tell my wife to throw me an event in downtown Atlanta. I had them tell her that I always wanted a gathering with my family and my friends together because it's never happened before. Well, my family got Heather on board, and they planned to all meet up in the lobby of the W Hotel in Buckhead.

I knew about all the planning and everything, so it

was fun to watch Heather try to keep this big "secret" from me. She realized we would get to the hotel before my family, so she tried to divert me to a drug store. I put up a fight to make it look like I didn't know what was going on. She decided to go to the bathroom, and stayed in there for a long time to try to take up time for my family to get there. I knew what was going on the entire time, so it was entertaining to say the least.

Finally, we get to the hotel. She gets out of the car and walks inside the lobby. As I walk in, everyone shouts, "Surprise!" I stand there like I didn't know what was going on. Heather knows I don't like surprises, so she immediately begins to blame my mother and my sister for the entire thing. It was so funny! Then, my sister told Heather to come closer to her. As she walked up and turned her back to me, I proceeded to get down on one knee.

When Heather turned around, I was down and presenting the ring to her. She put her hands over her face, dropped down in a squatting position, and she began to cry. My family and some folks were there to snap pictures and get some video footage. It was awesome. From that moment, there was no turning back. When Heather put the ring on her finger, the game started, and there was no end in sight. The engagement had officially begun.

That night, Heather began to talk about the wedding and all the things that needed to get done. I didn't know what I had just done. I didn't think anything about a ceremony, flowers, vows, family, friends, plane tickets, feeding people, tuxes, wedding gowns, make-up, engagement photos, gifts, etc. I was dumbfounded! For some reason I figured we were just going to find a church and get hitched. I didn't realize all the planning that would go in to the wedding ceremony. I had no clue what to expect with the engagement. Now that I've lived through it, I can freely share with you some of my experiences.

First, make sure that you always remember the purpose of why you're engaged. The engagement or betrothal is a promise to marry, and it's the period of time between proposal and marriage. During this time, the couple really begins to learn more about each other. Usually, this is the time of a great deal of planning.

When there is planning, there is usually some arguing to follow. There could be arguing over the colors, non-involvement on one of the person's behalf, spending too much money, not spending enough money, showing no interest, etc. The list is endless.

I'd recommend making sure the parents have met long before the engagement period. Proper etiquette is for the man to approach the woman's father, and to ask him for his daughter's hand in marriage. If the father agrees to it, the man is able to then ask the woman to be his wife.

After speaking with the father, it's polite for the parents of both the bride and the groom to meet, if they haven't already. During this time, the families should really begin to spend a great deal of time together and iron out any problems they may be experiencing. This is the time to recognize any "monster-in-law" type of problems. If those exist, I'd recommend having a heart-to-heart and properly laying down the law without being disrespectful or vengeful. You're fully committed now, so make sure the family is well aware of the commitment. Let them know that their words don't supersede the words of your spouse.

Sons, sit down and talk with your mother. Take care of the problem of an overbearing mother so your wife will not have to deal with it. You are tasked to leave your mother and your father and be joined with your wife, so make sure you communicate that separation to your mother.

Daughters, make sure you communicate the same thing to your father. Don't allow your father to be involved in your marriage, and don't allow him to dictate orders to your husband. Your father should deal with the matters of his home, and not try to dictate what happens in yours.

It's standard practice for the groom to purchase an engagement ring for the soon-to-be bride. I'd recommend not overspending on it. The significance of the union isn't based on the size of the ring; it's based on the pureness of the heart. Diamonds are a nice perk, but they're definitely not mandatory. No woman should put pressure on a man to purchase a ring that is outside of what he can afford. If a bride is so big on the size of the ring, as the groom, I'd sit her down and ask her to check her motives. This must be discussed, and it must be thoroughly dealt with before moving forward.

Nonetheless, if the bride accepts the ring, she is considered the fiancée. The man is considered the fiancé. For some, this can be a very overwhelming time, because of all the planning and things that go into the process.

The usual questions are, "Who do we tell first?", "What do we do first?" "How are we going to announce our engagement?" "Where are we going to get married?" These are some of the typical questions we ask one another when we have crossed that threshold of engagement.

It's always polite to tell the good news to the immediate family first like the mother, father, sister, brother, and children. Then, pass the message on to the grandparents, uncles, aunts, cousins, etc. Because of many of our family structures, the typical family isn't always made up of a father, mother, sister, brother, grandmother, and grandfather. There could be a close aunt or a very close cousin who is like a brother or sister to you.

Maybe you're not close with your parents, but you're extremely close with your grandparents. Either way, it's still polite to respect your parents, no matter how you feel about them, by letting them know the news. You don't have to sit on pins and needles waiting for their response. Just be polite in telling them; then, keep moving forward. Don't get caught up in who should know now and who should later. These are trivial things that could take your focus away from what's most important.

The Ceremony

Some may consider having a courthouse wedding or a small gathering at a chosen destination. That's fine. The most important thing is to not get caught up in the small things. Keep your mind focused on the main goal of an eternal union that glorifies God in everything the two of you do.

My wife and I chose to get married in a courtyard, and I must say that it was an awesome experience. Right before we got ready to kiss for the first time, there was a misty rain that began to fall on us. It was as if God was washing us gently. It was beautiful. Then, we had our reception in a ballroom of the home that was on the property. It was elegant, tasteful, simple, and classy. Those are the things that greatly define our union, and it shows the mixture of both of us.

The planning was stressful to say the very least. We had a "wedding planner" who told us God told her to help us. About half way through the process she bolted, but she still managed to find time to make it to our wedding. Yes, these things do happen.

My bride and I would sit down and discuss the plans even though I didn't want to talk about them. All I wanted to know was "HOW MUCH DOES IT COST?" The details were somewhat irrelevant. However, I stayed very much involved in the process so we were able to pick stuff out together, rather than trying to do it separately and then make decisions.

We got into plenty of arguments over the wedding plans, and it was stressful at times. I knew it was my responsibility to keep the focus where it should remain; an eternal union that glorifies God in everything we do. There would be times where the tension was so thick that I didn't even want to be around my bride. In those times, I would insist that we go out for dinner or sit and talk to air out our differences. It was my job to bring closure to the disagreements. There were times when I failed, but I refused to remain defeated. We would argue over having candles, picking up the flowers, the kind of cake we were going to have, etc. It was bananas. Towards the end of the engagement period, I was leaning more toward going to a courthouse and getting hitched. The whole ceremony thing was just becoming too much for me.

Nonetheless, we had our ceremony, and it was a beautiful one. My wife and I decided after the ceremony that if we had to do it all over again, we would have a destination wedding. We had wedding crashers even though it was supposed to be by invitation only. Thankfully, we had enough food and cake. Sadly, I didn't get to taste, hardly, any of it. The only piece of cake I tasted was what my wife fed me. I'll never forget getting to our suite after the wedding and looking for my cake I was sure someone wrapped for me. Well, that didn't happen! There was no cake for me! Needless to say, I was quite disappointed and slightly upset. I spent a good deal of money on the cake, so having at least one slice was important to me. Nonetheless, I like to go to other people's weddings and eat their cake to make up for what I didn't eat at mine. If you se me at your wedding, I'd advise you to hide your cake. I'm joking. Well, I'm kind of joking.

My wife and I had a pretty big wedding party. She had three matrons-of-honor, one maid-of-honor, and four bridesmaids. I had one best man and seven groomsmen. Looking back, I would've kept two and allowed the others to just attend the ceremony. The selection process wasn't one I was extremely proud of or would ever duplicate. Thankfully, my wife and I didn't have arguments concerning the wedding party.

Afterwards, we both agreed that we should've kept it as small as possible. Many of the men in my party were men I had situational friendships with. I knew it, but I still asked them to be in the wedding party. I'm grateful they agreed to do it, but I would never make that kind of mistake again.

I'd advise you not to fill your wedding party with a

bunch of situational friends. These are people who are in your life because certain situations call for it. Examples of situational friendships are work and school friendships. Think about it. You spend eight hours a day at work or at school. You're bound to develop relationships with someone at the office to pass time or to have someone to talk with. This doesn't mean that you're great friends. It only means that you have something in common. However, the relationship usually ends once the situation ends.

Many of the men in my wedding party were situational friendships. We were friends because we worked or served at our local church together. Once I left the church, the situation ended, and so did the friendship.

Honestly, most of the ceremony was a huge blur. It's so surreal when you're there. You have all of these people around you who want your attention for pictures and to converse. It can be a very demanding, and stressful, but it is definitely still a happy time. The most important thing is to remember the main goal, which is to form an eternal union that glorifies God in everything you do. Don't spend so much time focused on the wedding day that you forget about focusing on everything else that takes place afterwards. I remember telling my wife, "Babe, I'm not focused on the wedding day. I'm focused on the days after the wedding." The ceremony is great, but it should take a backseat to the ultimate goal of being a pure representation of Christ and His union with the Church.

Virgin Lips

God: "Son, how will you end this time together?"

Me: "I'm going to give her a kiss on the cheek and a hug and tell her to call me when she gets home."

God: "You haven't paid the price to kiss her yet. She doesn't belong to you. She still belongs to Me."

Me: "For real?"

{Heather comes out of the restroom and walks over to where I was standing}

Heather: "Hey, thanks for waiting on me!"

Me: "Hey, I was just thinking about how I was going to end this time together. I haven't earned the right to kiss you yet. I don't want to kiss you until the day we get married."

Heather (with a confused look on her face): "Ummm, okay. Cool!"

I just let you in on some of the conversation I had with God at the end of my first outing I had with Heather, my now-wife. It was in January of 2009 in Manhattan. I'll never forget that day. I took the subway for the FIRST time. This was a big deal, because I'm not a fan of public transportation. It's not that I think I'm above it. I just like to be in control of my environment, and you cannot control a public method of transportation. I can control who gets in my car, but I can't control who gets on the bus.

I've shared this dialogue with people before. Jaws usually drop until they ask me this one simple question, "So.......you didn't kiss her?" My response is always the same. "I didn't kiss her, and I didn't plan on kissing her until our wedding day."

The issue is not about the kiss. To me, it's much more than that. It's about setting a standard in our relationship. It's about giving Heather a reason to want to respect me as a man. I told her on our first outing that I wouldn't kiss her, and I remained true to that standard.

I remember telling my then-pastor about meeting up with her. I told him where we were going and everything. He tried to coach me on what to say and what to do. It was quite funny, and a little sad. I told him about everything because I wanted him to be sure of my actions. He was aware of who Heather was, so him meeting her wasn't something he needed to do again. I just wanted to make sure I had someone protecting our relationship.

I realized how beautiful Heather was, and I didn't want to go against my word. Sadly, most men say some things, but they do other things, and they do them on purpose. Little do they know that the woman they're in a relationship with is slowly losing respect for them. I didn't want this to happen with my relationship. I knew I wanted it to work, so I was willing to CRUCIFY my flesh. In doing so, I walked in a place of God-given leadership as a man. I TOOK the responsibility for the relationship. I put boundaries all over our relationship so we wouldn't be tempted beyond our ability.

Heather and I saw only one movie alone. To some that may be just silly; however, movies have the tendency to make you want to curl up next to the one you're with especially if you're a "touchy" person. We didn't hang out all night alone. Instead, we set a curfew for ourselves. We always went out with other people to remain accountable. We didn't sleep in the same bed. In fact, we didn't sleep under the same roof.

Due to us being long distance, we talked on the phone a lot. However, we had to be mature about our talk-time. We wouldn't foolishly talk to each other until 3:00 in the morning. Instead, we went to bed at an appropriate time. We weren't kids anymore. We had to put away the childish things, and we had to act like mature adults. That was the right thing to do. We fought against our emotions to the point of hurt. We HAD TO HONOR GOD because I WASN'T WILLING TO ALLOW THIS RELATIONSHIP TO FAIL! I'm the man, and I took FULL responsibility for it.

My mindset simply believes that no man should kiss his "potential" bride until their wedding day.

Some.....okay, a lot, of people will differ with me. That's fine. Let me explain my rationale here. Heather and I have built a relationship that is solid. It couldn't be built on flesh, even though we're very attracted to each other. We didn't allow for our emotions to let us end our evenings in a passionate kiss, just because we had just had a disagreement and were looking for a way to diffuse it. We made ourselves sit there and TALK. That made every part of my body cringe because, like most men, I HATE TO TALK! I couldn't just go hold her because I made her cry, and yes, I've made her cry. She couldn't just start rubbing on me when she said things that weren't very respectful, and yes, she's said some things that weren't respectful. We had to mature to the point where our emotions would not trump our effective means of communication.

God had a plan in telling me not to kiss my bride until the wedding day. He wanted me to keep the emotions and the sexual tension in the right place. I can't fool anyone. I'm a man, and I had sexual tension just like any other man. But, I refused to let that tension have me! I told Heather, "Sunshine, I know the machinery works. I don't need to lay together to test it out."

Ladies, choose a man who has standards. You wouldn't expect a man to go to the grocery store and just walk out with a carton of eggs would you? Why not? Well, he hasn't PAID THE PRICE for them yet. You would FULLY expect for him to go into the store, find the eggs, assure they are the right eggs, ensure they aren't broken, go to the register and properly purchase them with the right currency. He is PAYING A PRICE for those eggs.

It took energy and discipline for him to go to the store and do all of that. He had to make a CHOICE to do it. So, don't let a man tell you that he CAN'T do it. That's hogwash! He can do it, especially seeing that he has the Holy Spirit to help him! Now, if he isn't saved, that's a different story. He just has to make a choice!

Ladies, if you wouldn't let a man steal a carton of eggs without first PAYING THE PRICE for them, then don't let him think for one second that he can have *your* "eggs" without earning them.

Heather and I believe that relationships are

SERIOUS BUSINESS, and only serious singles, who are led by God, should seek to be in them. We weren't playing then, and we aren't playing now. God has standards, and we should follow them! It's time that we acknowledge those standards and honor God. I can tell you from experience that God will honor you when you honor Him!

I honored my bride at the altar by kissing her with my virgin lips. What will you do? Be bold. Be different. Be radical. Keep your virgin lips.

I am in no way a relationship guru. I don't have all the answers for all of the relationship problems that exist in the world. I'm simply a guy who was involved in some relationships that failed miserably. I learned from those failures, and I sought a new way of doing things. Finding that "new way" led me to so much more. That "new way," my friends, is God's way. It's a way of honoring Him with our bodies, sacrificing our lives to Him, denying our flesh daily, taking up our cross, and following Him wholeheartedly.

I'm sure you may think that there are many things in your past that you've done that make you a terrible person. I know I've done some horrible things. I think of my past, and I am disgusted by most of my actions. There are many people who like to remind me of my past, but I don't focus on my past. I focus on my future.

When satan tries to remind me of my past, I quickly remind him of his future. His future is not too bright. The people who remind you of your past prove that they have too much time on their hands. They're so concentrated on your past mistakes that they've forgotten to repent of their own sins.

I had a family member who said, "I want to remind you where you came from." Well, I hate to break this to you, but I'm not trying to remember where I came from because I'm headed in a different direction. My future is not dependent on my past. If God forgets it, why should I try to remember it?

I am a new creature, and the blood of Jesus has cleansed me. My sins have been forgiven, and I am saved. This means that I live differently than people who are not saved. See, God is holy, and He desires for me to be holy. Does that mean I'm perfect? Absolutely not; however, it does mean that we have the opportunity to believe in the power of the One who is perfect *and continue to strive towards perfection.* His name is Jesus.

Does the fact I'm not perfect give me a reason to continue in sin? Absolutely not! I should continue in righteousness with the help of the Holy Spirit. Does the truth of grace mean I should continue in sin? Absolutely not! Grace is never an excuse to sin. Instead, it's a reason to abstain from it.

What happened to the days of holiness? What happened to the older women who taught the younger women about modesty, respecting their husbands, how to cook, and how to care for her children?

What happened to the older men who trained the younger men, instead of trying to exploit them for their personal gain? What happened to the preacher who stands boldly in the pulpit preaching a dynamic message on holiness and purity? When did compromise become so acceptable in the Church? How long will the Church sleep? How long will you sleep? Do you realize that you have a part to play in this life? That part begins with your personal relationship with Christ and the spreading of that relationship with others.

"Cornelius, I've already kissed or had sex with my future spouse. What should I do?" I'm glad you asked! I want to lay out some things that were on my heart concerning those people who may have the desire to begin to honor God with their relationship AFTER they have spent time kissing, having sex, engaging in foreplay, etc.

I don't dare desire for anyone to feel condemned by their past relationships; however, it is my desire that the Holy Spirit would convict you so that you are able to make wise decisions in the future. Do I believe a relationship can be restored after it has been tainted? I absolutely do! I don't care how many routes you find to get you from point A to point B. The objective is to find the route that is pleasing and honorable to God. If you've diverted off that route, it's time to simply get back on it and drive to the appointed destination. It's not deep at all.

No one needs to come lay hands on you or shout, "Jesus!" over you 7 times. Allow for the power of God to convict you, and allow for Him to make a mighty change in your life. Let the perfect work He begins in you come to completion. Don't try to do all the "good" things. Don't try to be a "good" boy or a "good" girl. Instead, focus in on glorifying God, learning His ways, not conforming yourself to the world, etc. Ask yourself these questions:

- Who have I allowed to teach me about relationships?

- Who are my examples of successful relationships?

- Have I taken what I know from the world and tried to make it applicable to the Kingdom of God?

- Have I asked God to give me a desire to glorify Him even though my flesh doesn't desire it?

- Are the people who I take advice from getting counsel from God?

Here are three things I'd like to share with those who are considering starting this successful journey towards a marriage that will glorify God.

1. **Change your mindset**. Romans 12:1,2 says *"I beseech you therefore, brethren, by the mercies of*

God, that ye present your bodies a living sacrifice, holy, acceptable unto God, which is your reasonable service. And be not conformed to this world: but be ye transformed by the renewing of your mind, that ye may prove what is that good, and acceptable, and perfect, will of God." These have to be some of my favorite verses from the Bible. They are packed with so much truth and depth. You can clearly see that Paul is instructing the Greeks to present their bodies as living sacrifices to God. My friends, we need to do the same. Paul then tells them to be transformed. How are they to be transformed? It's by the renewing of their mind. Why do they need to be transformed? It's so that they can prove what is that perfect and acceptable will of God. This is powerful. In our lives, we should focus on being transformed by learning the ways of God, listening to sermons that properly teach the truth without any deviation, consult wise counsel about the ways of the Lord, and continue to stay in constant communion with God. Most times, my wife and I are confronted with people who tell us that what we did is great, but they either don't agree or they don't think it takes all that. I hate to break this to you, but truth is truth no matter how you slay it. A cat is a cat even if you try to dress it up to look like a dog. Don't choose to live your life based on how you feel about things. Do what the Bereans did in Acts 17:11 and "… *{Search} the scriptures daily {to find out} whether {these} things are true.*"

I dare you to search the heart of God and ask Him if this is His desire. I warn you not to allow your flesh to dictate your searching of the truth. Going to a preacher is fine, but I wouldn't trust my bottom dollar on another man's interpretation of what he thinks it means. I wouldn't dare want to trust a man who simply eisegetes the Word and fails to properly exegete it.

2. **Communicate the desire of the relationship.** Don't leave anything to chance or open to confusion. I sat down with my wife and I spoke to her about the

boundaries we needed to set in our relationship. A good leader learns that communication is extremely important. He knows it's in "what" he says and "how" he says it. I'd advise you to sit down with the person you're in a relationship with and communicate the boundaries. Talk about the desires that are on your hearts. Discuss the ending goal of the relationship. Most times, this can give you great insight to the future. If you sit down with your friend and he tells you that he doesn't see himself getting married right now, you know you should probably make an adjustment depending on how you feel about the situation. If the relationship lacks purpose, abuse is inevitable. Sit down and talk with each other.

3. **Discuss who you will be accountable to with each other.** Make sure you are accountable to people who are **willing** and **able** to assist you. It's not wise for a man who's struggling with a crack addiction to hold you accountable for your crack

addition. His addiction shows you that he's already vulnerable and he's tempted with what tempts you. This doesn't mean he cannot be a friend, but it does mean you should consider searching for someone else to hold you accountable.

Here's a key thing about accountability. Accountability is useless if there is no transparency! You must be willing to be open. You have to open yourself, and your possible spouse, up to possible rebuke and scrutiny. Accountability takes a great deal of humility. I have a "Pocket of Accountability". This small group of guys knows about my struggles and my downfalls. I trust them with my life! I've opened my life to them, so that they can rebuke, encourage, etc. They are whom I call when I'm frustrated or happy. They see me at my worst, and they are there when I'm at my best. They see the side of me that the rest of the world cannot see.

During our journey to marriage, my wife and I had couples that we were accountable to. They helped us, advised us, talked with us, fellowshipped with us, etc. I wouldn't dare go to a single man and ask him to advise me on my relationship. I'm sure the single man has great knowledge, but the knowledge he possesses doesn't have a firm foundation unless he has some kind of experience. It's no secret that a single man thinks like a single man. That's because he's single. He only has to care for himself. His mind leans more towards selfishness because he is all he has to deal with, daily. He doesn't have a wife to be concerned with like Paul mentions in 1 Corinthians 7:33.

4. **Involve your family, friends, and fellowship groups**. I'm a firm believer that dating is crippling our society. The idea of dating is so worldly and individualistic. Think about it. Usually, it's a guy and a girl who desire to be in a relationship. The two enter into that relationship with the mindset that they can walk alone, just the two of them, on their way to marriage. Along the way, the guy and the girl will go to the

movies, go to late dinners, etc. They'll begin to talk about stuff that isn't edifying to each other, their parents, or God. Since no one monitors their relationship, they are free to do as they wish all in the bounds of their ignorance. We make a fatal mistake by not including our parents, our pastor, our friends, etc. in the decision-making process. I want you to understand that marriage is forever, so no one should enter it lightly. A young woman should make sure her father, who has authority over her, is kept in the process of the relationship. The father, who will eventually give his daughter away, should be an intricate part of the process. Most times, the father is either absent, ignorant, or silent. Either way, you should not skip over the sanctity that is found in protection. Ladies, allow the man to be scrutinized by your family, friends, pastor, etc. Allow for them to ask him questions and learn of his past. Bring him over to dinner, and allow him to sit and eat with you and your family. Tell him that the way to your heart is through your father, either earthly or

Heavenly. Either way, don't try to tame a man alone.

Fellas, make sure you respect her by introducing yourself to the people in her life whom she respects. Sit with them. Learn of her. Allow them to ask you questions. Don't be afraid to go out in groups.

It's important that both of you begin to notice things about each other that are going to be very noticeable in marriage. Notice how she is rude to everyone in her family. If she doesn't respect her father, there's a good chance she won't respect you. If she doesn't listen to the voice of God and follow His word, there's a great chance she will not listen to you. If she doesn't have the desire to submit to God, there's a good chance that she will not submit to you either. This is truth, my friends. Therefore, include your family, your friends, your pastor, your deacons, your elders, etc. in the walk towards the altar.

Please make sure that you use wisdom though. If you know your family isn't prepared to deal wisely in the ways of

Scripture because of their unwillingness or ignorance, don't be so sure to take their advice. Bottom line: I don't take counsel from anyone who doesn't take counsel from God.

5. **Don't be afraid to lead**. This one is dedicated to the guys. I understand that we live in a society where women have been forced to lead because the men are too sorry, too uneducated, too passive, etc. to do so. Ladies, I applaud your efforts; however, I hate that you've had to take that position. In the Kingdom of God, man is the head of woman. In marriage, the husband is the head of the wife. This is not to be domineering; rather, it's to maintain order. Anything with two heads is a monster!

   I understand that you are not married yet; however, I ask that the man be man enough to lead. He must be willing and able to provide a path for his one-day wife to walk on so that she doesn't stumble and fall. It is the job of the husband to love his wife as Christ loved the Church. Christ made it easy for the Church while He took the pain, sin, misery, etc. That's love!

Ladies, the man in your life is supposed to do the same thing. He is to make the journey so easy for you, that all you have to do is walk – even with your eyes closed. The man must understand that Christ is his head; therefore, he must be led of God. His decisions must be sound, prudent, holy, and firm. He must not allow anyone to intrude in the relationship. He must give respect to her father, both earthly and Heavenly, and he must be bold in everything he chooses to do.

Here are some of the things I did to ensure I remained true to my word.

1. **Conducted the relationship like an adult**. Like most people, I've been in relationships that didn't go so great. It was partly because I acted like a complete fool and I was led by what I didn't know. The Holy Spirit helped me realize that it's difficult to win a game of basketball while using baseball rules. That

means that I couldn't be successful in this relationship by using what I knew from my failed relationships.

Here's the thing, my relationships failed in the past; therefore, why would I want to use the same failed methods? That makes no sense at all! I told my wife that I didn't want to conduct the relationship like we were still in grade school. You know how we used to do it. We would want to stay on the phone all night just to hear the other person breathing or until someone went to sleep. I just wasn't going to do it. I've done it, but I'd matured beyond that.

Since our relationship was long distance, we had to talk on the phone. That was our way of communication. Nonetheless, we had to be mature about the decisions we were making. It was foolish to sit on the phone until 4am knowing that we both had to get up and go to work the next morning. It would have been foolish to sit around texting all day when we knew that there was important work to be done. We could not allow for the relationship to push aside all of the other things God instructed both of us to do. We also knew that the relationship could not become more important than our relationship with God. I could not substitute my time on the phone with Heather, for my time I should be spending with God. That's just unacceptable.

2. **I took responsibility**. I made sure we remained accountable to someone at all times. You'll notice I said "I made sure." The reason I say that is because "I" took responsibility for the relationship. I realized her father was deceased, so I knew I needed to be extra careful not to ruin someone who didn't belong to me. I believe it is a man's responsibility to provide a path for a woman to follow. I believe the man must take responsibility for the relationship, especially in case where the father is either deceased, absent, or silent! The man cannot do this alone. He must be lead by God, and he must be empowered through and by the inner working of the Holy Spirit.

If the man is not saved, the Holy Spirit doesn't dwell in him; therefore, he will rely on will power. Unfortunately, as I stated before, will has no power! I would oftentimes tell my wife that we couldn't do certain things people in worldly relationships would do, such as, go to the movie late, go out eating late, sleep in the same house or in the same bed, etc.

Heather and I went to one movie alone, and she clowned me the entire time because we went at like 12:30pm. We were the only young couple there. I did that on purpose though. I wanted to go to an early movie so we weren't around a bunch of horny adolescents rubbing and touching on each other. I didn't need any more temptation than what was already raging in me. We didn't go out to eat late unless there was another couple going with us or meeting us there.

When Heather came down to Atlanta, she would stay at my house, and I would go stay with a friend. When I left my friend's house, I told him where I was going and what time he could expect me back. There was one time that I was late coming back to his house, so he called me to, "check on me to see where I was located." It just so happened that dinner ran longer than I expected, so it took a little longer to get back home. I knew I would have to make some unpopular decisions in my relationship; however, that is the responsibility of every leader. A woman shouldn't have to wait for a man to lead or set an easy path for her to walk. My goal wasn't to be Heather's father. It was to make her way easy just like Christ did for the Church. I wanted to show her that I could take responsibility then so when we were married it would be a continuation of what she already knew.

3. **Kept the touching at a minimum**. If you've ever spoken to my wife about our relationship, I'm sure she has told you about the "church hugs" I gave her for about a year. Those are the hugs where you bring the person in at the shoulder and pat them on the other shoulder. Here's the thing: I knew the equipment worked, so there was no use trying to test it out. My wife is VERY beautiful, so I knew the close hugs weren't going to do it for me. I didn't need her putting her breasts all on my chest or coming so close that she could feel the imprint of.....well, you know where that's going. *cough* *cough* I knew that

touching had to remain at a minimum. That was difficult for my wife because she LOVES to touch. She's a very affectionate person, and that's how she was raised. Even knowing this, I didn't allow her to put her hand on my chest, lay on my chest, touch me on my thigh, give tight hugs, etc.

To some, that my sound extreme, but, for me, it was the right thing to do. Again, she wasn't officially my wife. I wouldn't go out and just hug up on some woman I met on the street unless I was a complete pervert. I knew touching would lead to something, so I made sure we kept it at a minimum. We did hold hands. We did give each other "church hugs", but that was as far as I was willing to go for a long time. We didn't cuddle and watch movies either. Our engagement photos made us both very uncomfortable because we had never been that close to each other. If you notice in our photos, we did not kiss either. Being that close to her face was very uncomfortable. Now, seeing that we're married, being close to her is my delight.

4. **We remained accountable to someone at all times**. The first time Heather and I went to have dinner, alone, was in New York. We went to this vegan restaurant in Manhattan. I remember I had something that tasted pretty darn close to bird seeds. It was gross, but being with her made it all the best. Before I went to meet her, I spoke about it with my then-pastor. He was totally fine with me going. He knew what time I was returning back to the residence, so I left. When I got back, we talked about the evening. I told him everything to make sure I wasn't doing something wrong. I really wanted to make sure I was doing everything right this time.

I'll never forget when I told him I wasn't going to kiss her. He looked at me shocked and said, "God told me that you would get married soon then". He was joking! He was somewhat right though. As I stated earlier, when Heather flew down from New York to Atlanta, she would stay in my house, and I would go to a friend's house. For a couple of months previous to that, she would come down and she would stay in a hotel and rent a car. I didn't want her to stay in my house because I didn't know her like that. I wasn't going to give my house to just anyone. I knew she was my wife, but I just wanted to make sure, if you know what I'm saying. We made sure we went out in groups. We made sure we didn't sleep in the same bed. We made sure someone was always around us. We made sure were always covered.

Accountability is important. We're a family; a BODY. The right arm of the body isn't independent of the shoulder. They must work together. The same is true for us. We must work together by bearing one another's burdens, confessing our faults to one another, and being truthful about where we fall. I wanted this relationship to work, so I was willing to do whatever I had to do to make it work.

5. **Stayed in constant fellowship with the Holy Spirit**. Hey, if I've made you think I was capable of doing this on my own, forgive me! I wasn't and am not capable of doing this on my own. I needed the help and guidance of the Holy Spirit. There were

times I would wake up early and spend time with Him, because I know what my body desired. There were times I would fast so that my body knew that it didn't control me. It was during this time that I realized the power of fasting. It helped me to keep my body in subjection, and I desperately needed it.

There were times when the Holy Spirit would speak to me on my way home about what to do or what to say when I spoke with Heather. He led our relationship. We cannot take any credit for His work. He is to be glorified by all of it! There were times that Heather wanted to buy plane tickets to come to Atlanta to see me. I would tell her to wait, based on what the Holy Spirit would tell me. Can you believe that she would wait, only to find a cheaper flight that fit the times she had initially wanted to fly down? That gave her confidence in knowing that I knew how to listen to the voice of God, rather than my emotions. She was able to see firsthand that my relationship with God wasn't just some "fly-by-night", "Johnny-come-lately" kind of deal. She knew I was serious about my relationship with Him above all else. He is to get all glory out of this; not us.

We really want people to hear and get this testimony so we can curb a lot of terrible relationships, unexpected pregnancies, adulteries, etc. plaguing our society. The liberalism of our society cannot be blamed on liberal politicians; rather, we should also look at the ministers who have been assigned to preach and live out the Gospel around the world. This, my friends, is a part of the Good News. Without the life, death and resurrection of Christ, none of this would be possible.

I can understand if you don't want to conduct your relationship in the ways I've described. I've heard countless times that people know other people who've done it another way and their marriage is just great. That's awesome. My grandfather once told me that there's two ways to skin a catfish; a long, confusing way, or an easy, disciplined way. Either way, you'll skin it.

Our prayer is that you don't choose the long, confusing way. Don't choose the way that will lead to heartache, emotional roller coasters, broken relationships, unexpected pregnancies, etc. Choose the way that leads to life, discipline, structure, humility, etc. I've presented you with two paths; choose one.

'Til Death Do Us Part

I pray that what you've read thus far has helped you as much as it has encouraged me while writing it. I really want you to take some time and focus on everything you read in this last chapter. Don't just skim the words. Really allow these words to settle in your heart. Read this chapter over and over again if you have to do so. Don't let this pass you by because of oversight.

The Christian marriage between a man and a woman is likened to the marriage between Christ and the Church. We recognize the Church as each and every believer around this world. They are the "sent out ones" who are called by God to share the Gospel abroad.

When they come together, they form one of the most powerful associations this world has every seen, because they are founded on one faith, by one Savior, sharing one message, all in unison. We recognize Jesus to be "the Anointed One." He is Jesus, the Savior of all mankind. He is the world's last hope of redemption and salvation. He is the only way to God, and all men will bow their knees to worship and serve Him.

Now, when Jesus joins in union with the Church, He requires that the Church come before Him and die. This means the Church must let go of their plans, actions, desires, and thoughts so that they can humbly submit to His. Marriage is no different. When a woman is joined in holy union with her husband, she must come before him and relinquish her own will and desires for the plans God has set in place for the union. She, like the Church, comes before her groom ready to accept his identity, and to die to her own.

I know this is a tough pill to swallow, especially in the hedonistic society we live in nowadays. Media and print constantly send messages throughout the day urging women to be independent and totally counter-

Christ. Ladies, I stand with a remnant few who ask that you become counter-culture and truly take your place in the rightful union of sacred marriage with your husband. I'm constantly told by women that they fear submission because they're afraid they will lose their identity. I hate to break this to you, but your identity must die.

When a man takes a woman in marriage, her identity and his identity become one. It is written "The two will become one." The two will join one another in sacred union under the identity of the groom. This is why the minister calls out the groom and bride as Mr. and Mrs. (Insert groom's last name here). They are not two separate people after the ceremony. Their spirit is knit together by the hand of God and a needle of love. Their soul, thoughts, will, plans, etc. all become one over time.

How do they become one? Well, there is but one truth, one faith, one hope, one Savior, and one sacrifice. The two must believe in the same truth, the same faith, the same hope, the same Savior, and the same sacrifice. Their mutual belief in the same truth serves as the glue that binds the two together.

Since their hope is in the same thing, and they both believe the same truth, they have no other choice but to become one. From the time the two come to know one another, they are two free-flowing ships making their way to the same dock. Upon docking, they disembark their separate ships and begin a journey as one with the guidance of God the Spirit, the protection of God the Father, and the saving power of God the Son.

A bride must work earnestly to surrender herself to being washed by the Word of God and cleansed from all of her wicked and malicious thinking. The same is true for Christ and the Church. The Church must surrender to the ways and plans of the Groom, Jesus Christ. Anything outside the perfect union and submission of that union is adultery, and it must be avoided. This cannot be just some phony show of submission either. It must be real; and if it is real, it will bear fruit. If it is not, it will bear fruit. Either way, it will bear fruit.

After I was engaged to my now-wife, I would ask her to do things that were against what she wanted to do. There would be times where she would want to argue or question the decision. There were even times where she would tell me she wasn't going to do it. Then, there were times where she would look at me and tell me that she was going to go ahead and do it. Little did I know that she wasn't really excited about doing them. There were even times where she expressed that she didn't really want to do it. She referred to it as "false submission." This is where she gave off the image of submission, but she was still telling herself that she wasn't interested in doing what she was asked to do. That was a breakthrough moment for our marriage because I didn't really realize that was what she was doing.

There were times where I would conclude that that may be the problem, but I really didn't have proof of it. Here's the thing: If her submission weren't real, time and pressure would prove it. You can dress a cat to look like a dog. You can teach it how to bark. You can feed it dog food. You can even give it a dog name. Unfortunately, it will always be a cat. The cat's nature will always show through, and it will soon show its true colors.

The most important thing to realize is that when you come together to be married and you join in that sacred union, you must come ready to die. Anything with two heads is a monster, and a building built on multiple foundations can't stand. The two must become one. If not, the union is in rebellion and out of order. A man who claims to be a Christian is a liar if his life doesn't mature to resemble the life of Christ. This is true for marriage also. A bride is a liar if her will doesn't fall in line with the will of the one to whom she has been joined. She carries the title, but her heart is far from the truth.

As for the groom, he is to give his entire life and being over to the will and calling of the Lord. He is to become a student of the perfect Master, and not be conformed to this world. He is to take on the head of Christ and begin to think as if He was Christ. His foundation must be unconditional love, grace, and mercy. He is to give himself over to spiritual exercises that grow his faith and encourage his union with Christ. Those exercises include prayer, fasting, consecration, giving to others, etc. He isn't in the marriage to dominate his wife or his children by law, but that doesn't mean he should discount law altogether.

This is why it's dangerous for a woman to marry a man who isn't saved or being renewed spiritually. The religious man will use his warped and perverse heart to rule his law by law. He yells at his wife and tells her that she has to do what he says because he is a "man" and a "leader." Grooms, any man who has to convince himself and others that he is a man, isn't a man at all. He's a little boy who's crying out for attention.

It's not enough for a woman to just marry a man because he "goes to church," sings in the choir, ushers on Sunday mornings, joins with the "vision keepers," or tithes. She should allow her father, or whoever is seen as the counsel over the union to see if the man is who he says he is. I would be a fool to go and buy a tree without first checking its' fruit. I would want to know if the tree is producing the type of fruit I desire, and I want to know if the fruit that's produced is maturing and ripening. If the fruit is stagnant and getting wormy, it's evident the tree is going bad and it must be discarded. This is wisdom, and it cannot be ignored.

Folks, your marriage is going to be tested in every area. You will have disagreements and arguments. Here's the thing: Dead people don't argue. As the two of you come together, realize that you're both dead to arguing, malicious thoughts against one another, and hateful ways. Realize that you're dead to selfishness, and you're alive to love, grace and mercy.

Do everything in your power to keep peace in your home. Don't allow anyone or anything to rob you of your peace. Keep troublesome family members out of your marriage. Keep Christ as the focus of the marriage, and don't allow anyone or anything to destroy the union God is forming between the both of you.

Pray together as much as possible. Spend as much time together as you can. Work out your differences, and don't allow trivial issues to stop you from maturing in your union. Understand that it's not all about you anymore. You are joining, or have joined, in union with your spouse. Wives, submit to your husbands. Husbands, love your wives. This is the will of God concerning our marriages.

So, you still want to be married?

God bless you.

Appendix

PAST

◈ The best part about my childhood was?

◈ The worst part about my childhood was?

◈ The scariest thing that ever happened to me was?

◈ Something I'm afraid to tell anyone about my past is?

◈ A past situation that could affect my future is?

◈ The way I feel about my past relationship history is?

◈ My biggest fears in life are?

◈ My biggest needs in life are?

◈ My most frequent mood is?

◈ The thing I hate most is?

◈ The thing I worry about most is?

◈ Three things I want to change about

myself are?

◈ Three things I really like about myself are?

◈ My most common daydream is?

◈ I get angry when?

◈ My favorite kind of house pet is?

◈ My overall opinion about myself is?

◈ I think my greatest personality asset is?

◈ My greatest personality weakness is?

◈ I find the greatest enjoyment in?

◈ The sin I struggle most with is?

◈ I'm most ashamed about?

◈ Someone I greatly admire is?

◈ The way I feel about death is?

◈ I think war is?

◈ I feel happy when?

◈ I have no use for people who?

◈ When someone acts rude to me, I?

◈ When someone is unfair, I?

◈ I feel jealous of?

◈ My dream vacation would include?

◈ The things I find the most fun are?

✧ My favorite sport(s) is?

✧ Playing sports in my future is a _____ on a scale from one to ten.

✧ Watching sports on T.V. is a _____ for me on a scale from one to ten.

✧ I am disgusted by?

✧ When I am afraid (substitute sad, angry, happy, lonely, tired), I?

✧ My hobbies include?

✧ I spend _____ hours a week at my hobbies.

✧ What I really want when I am sick is?

✧ The part of my body I am most bothered by is?

✧ The part of my body I am most happy with is?

✧ What hurts me most is?

✧ The best (and worst) thing about life is?

✧ The first thing I notice about someone is?

✧ When someone is angry with me, I?

✧ When someone is disappointed in me, I?

◇ The worst (and best) thing about the opposite sex is?

◇ Being teachable means?

◇ People (including me) should say they're sorry when?

MARRIAGE.

◈ My reasons for wanting to get married are?

◈ I think the keys to a good marriage are?

◈ The biggest mistakes I made in past relationships are?

◈ The area I've grown the most in relationships is?

◈ Relationships in the past have taught me?

◈ I've always viewed marriage as?

◈ My parents had a _____ marriage.

◈ I learned _____ about marriage from my parents.

◈ I think the things in marriage you should be honest about are?

◈ The areas I'm concerned about being married are?

- ⬦ The areas I'm excited about being married are?
- ⬦ Marriage for me will be giving up?
- ⬦ Marriage for me will be gaining?
- ⬦ I think separate vacations are?
- ⬦ Traveling together is?
- ⬦ When having conflict, I like to: cool off by myself before discussing the problem; discuss and work the problem out right. away; pretend there is no problem and just move on; analyze the problem as to what it is, why it happened, how to avoid it in the future, etc?
- ⬦ Arguing and or fighting is?
- ⬦ The best way to handle disagreements is to?
- ⬦ What I fear most about marriage is?
- ⬦ What I anticipate most about marriage is?
- ⬦ The role of in-laws in marriage is?
- ⬦ The thing that will make me most secure (and insecure) in marriage is?

⬦ Dating (each other) after you are married is?

⬦ Love is?

⬦ "Till death do us part" means?

⬦ I think people should be allowed to divorce when?

⬦ For me, divorce is?

SEX

◇ I think sex is/will be?

◇ I think a healthy marriage involves sex [ ]
per week or _____ per month.

◇ I'm aware that real sex in marriage differs
from Hollywood in the following ways?

◇ I think being naked in front of someone
is?

◇ On a scale from one to ten, sex is a
_____ in importance in a good
marriage for me.

◇ What sex means to me is?

◇ Being spontaneous or creative in
marriage sex sounds?

MONEY/FINANCES

◈ I think money is?

◈ Spending money is hard/easy for me because?

◈ The biggest waste of money is?

◈ The best investment of money is?

◈ I have _____ in personal debt.

◈ I use credit cards for?

◈ I think car loans are?

◈ Saving up to buy big ticket items is?

◈ My savings plan is?

◈ My retirement plan is?

◈ The way I feel about tithing is?

◈ I hope my spouse is a: saver, spender, somewhere in between.

◈ On a scale from one to ten, financial security is _____ in importance to me.

◈ I want to save up to buy a?

◈ The kind of house I want to own someday is?

◈ Other items I hope to own are?

◈ Charities I want to contribute to are?

PHYSICAL APPEARANCE

◇ Is my own appearance important to me?

◇ Is it important that my spouse maintains his/her current physical appearance/weight throughout our marriage?

◇ How important is hygiene to me, i.e. brushing teeth, taking showers, deodorant, etc.?

◇ How do I like to dress for special occasions? For church? For dates? For work?

◇ Do I want to be able to have a say in my spouse's choice of clothing, hairstyle, or general appearance?

◇ Do I care if they have a say in mine?

◇ Is cologne/perfume important to me?*

◈ What physical features are attractive to me?

HOUSEHOLD

◇ How clean is a home that is comfortable for me?

◇ What is my favorite thing about home?

◇ What can I not tolerate in my home (noise, clutter, dirt, pets, unmade beds, etc.)?

◇ How many/which jobs do I think I should do to keep my house maintained?

◇ How many/which jobs do I think my spouse should do around the house?

◇ Who should keep the yard maintained (spouse, both, or hired out)?

◇ Who will maintain the cars (spouse, both, or hired out)?

◇ Who will make decisions for and carry out decorating the home (spouse, both, hired out)?

◇ Who will cook family meals?

◇ How many meals do I expect to cook or for my spouse to cook daily?

◇ Who will do the shopping?

◇ Who will do laundry?

◇ Who will do the dishes?

◇ Who will pay bills?

RECREATION

◈ My idea of recreation is?

◈ To me, camping means?

◈ My favorite sports are?

◈ The way I relax on the weekends is by?

◈ What areas of recreation do I want my spouse to accompany me on?

◈ What areas of recreation do I want to do with my friends or alone?

◈ How often will I want to spend time away from the family in my own recreation?

KIDS

- ◈ I think kids are?
- ◈ Kids get on my nerves when they?
- ◈ I love it when kids?
- ◈ The way I feel about other people's kids is?
- ◈ The way kids usually feel about me is?
- ◈ Kids should be disciplined when?
- ◈ The way I want to discipline my kids is?
- ◈ The role of a parent is?
- ◈ I want _____ kids someday.
- ◈ How important is showing physical affection to my kids?
- ◈ Is telling my kids I love them important?
- ◈ How much time do I think I should spend with my kids daily?

✧ How important is two-parent interaction and discipline?

✧ I think the bottom line for discipline should be with the (mom or dad)?

✧ How important is it for kids to respect their parents in my home?

✧ When it comes to discipline, I think I will be: lenient, strict, or somewhere in-between?

✧ Where do I want my kids educated (private school, Christian school, home school, etc.)?

HEALTH/HISTORY

◈ Taking care of myself and my health is
_____ important to me.

◈ I think a healthy lifestyle includes?

◈ Physical exercise is?

◈ To me, eating right means?

◈ My idea of a good work out is?

◈ My life fitness plan is to?

◈ My health problems (present or past) are?

◈ I take medication for?

◈ I think life long-term supports are?

◈ People in my family have a history of the
following health problems?

◈ People in my family have died at the ages
of?

INTIMACY

◈ I feel loved when?

◈ The way I show love to people is?

◈ Which of the following are ways I feel most loved? Time spent with, words of encouragement/praise, gifts, being touched and hugged in a non-sexual manner, when people do things for (serve) me.

◈ Showing affection in front of kids or friends is?

◈ Intimacy is developed through?

◈ I think a good marriage needs at least _____ hours a day (or week) of focused communication to stay connected.

WORK

◇ My idea of a dream job is?

◇ I think the average number of hours a person can regularly work a week and maintain family commitment is?

◇ Providing for the family is whose responsibility?

◇ My career plans are?

◇ How important is a steady job to me?

◇ What kind of work ethic do I want in my mate?

◇ Where do I draw the line with a job that demands too much time?

◇ My plans for retirement are?

SPIRITUALITY/RELIGION

◇ The way I feel about God is?

◇ I think the way God feels about me is?

◇ On a scale of one to ten, going to church is _____ in importance for my life and future.

◇ I want to raise my kids in the _____ faith.

◇ Will God be the center of my home? Why or why not?

◇ If yes, how will I make Him the center?

◇ Prayer is something I do when?

◇ To me, the Bible is?

◇ Other religions besides Christianity are?

◇ Eternal life is accomplished by?

◇ Select and discuss the following. To me, God is: personal, real, distant, vague, angry, happy, loving, harsh, demanding, gentle, kind, good, make-believe, living, powerful, weak, or other.

◇ The way to have a relationship with God is?

◇ For me, including God in my daily life is?

◇ On a scale from one to ten, obeying God and His word is a _____ to me.

◇ When I die, I?

Made in the USA
Charleston, SC
14 January 2014